NON-CUSTODIAL SANCTIONS

ALTERNATIVE MODELS
FOR POST-COMMUNIST SOCIETIES

Non-Custodial Sanctions

Alternative Models
For Post-Communist Societies

Tiberiu Dianu

Nova Science Publishers, Inc.
New York

Assistant Vice President/Art Director: Maria Ester Hawrys
Office Manager: Annette Hellinger
Graphics: Frank Grucci
Acquisitions Editor: Tatiana Shohov
Book Production: Ludmila Kwartiroff, Christine Mathosian,
               Maria A. Olmsted and Tammy Sauter
Editorial Production: Susan Boriotti
Circulation: Cathy DeGregory and Maryanne Schmidt

Library of Congress Cataloging-in-Publication Data available upon request

ISBN 1-56072-509-5

Copyright © 1997 by   Nova Science Publishers, Inc.
                6080 Jericho Turnpike, Suite 207
                Commack, New York 11725
                Tele. 516-499-3103   Fax 516-499-3146
                E-Mail: Novascience@earthlink.net
                Web Site: http://www.nexusworld.com/nova

Printed in the United States of America

To An-Chi,
who made my dreams come true

CONTENTS

ABOUT THE AUTHOR

Tiberiu Dianu (1961-) is a graduate of the Bucharest University, (LL.B. 1985, M.A. 1987 in Criminology, M.Sc. 1990 in Criminal Justice, doctoral studies), the Manchester University (M.Phil. 1996 in Criminal Justice), the American University at Washington DC (LL.M. 1997 in International Legal Studies), and a Visiting Scholar of the Strasbourg University (1990) and the Oxford University (1994). Between 1985-1995, he practiced law in Romania as an attorney, judge, senior counselor, lecturer and senior researcher for the Judiciary and academia, and as a legal adviser for various Romanian and American non-government organizations.

He has authored several monographs and over 60 studies and articles on law, human rights and sociology, published in Romania, the United States, the Netherlands, and Hungary. Recent books in English include *Constitution of Romania 1991: A Critical Approach* (1997) and *International Penal Protection of Human Rights* (1996).

LIST OF TABLES

FOREWORD

Non-Custodial Sanctions by Tiberiu Dianu is a comprehensive, scholarly and exhaustive review of the effectiveness of various models, alternative to prison, used at the pre-trial, sentencing and post-detention stages in various justice systems around the world. It is an impressive and well-documented work that covers all the major criminal justice approaches and systems, worldwide. The result of extensive research, careful documentation, and rigorous analysis, this volume represents a major contribution to comparative justice studies. The author demonstrates superb research skills, excellent command of the international literature, and strong analytical capabilities. His major objective is to provide options derived from worldwide practices for reforming the criminal justice systems of Eastern European countries. He succeeds remarkably well in providing such assessments and models. Moreover, he offers an instructive, useful, and captivating survey of various approaches and practices in different parts of the world.

This work will be very useful to students, scholars, and practitioners alike, particularly as it presents such a comprehensive and well-written comparative panorama of justice systems' alternatives to imprisonment. While its title may seem to limit its scope and impact to Eastern and Central Europe, it actually encompasses all continents. It will be useful reading for all those who are genuinely interested and committed to criminal justice reform in all corners of the world. This work is definitely a major contribution to the comparative justice literature and will make a major impact and a definitive contribution to criminal justice reform and innovation, worldwide.

Emilio Viano
Professor of Justice, Law and Society
American University
Washington, DC

PREFACE

Non-Custodial Sanctions approaches, from a meta-analytical perspective, the effectiveness of various alternative models used in pre-trial, sentencing process and post-detention, with a focus on probation. The project has been motivated by the need of finding feasible substitutes to imprisonment, in order to be efficiently implemented within the statutory law of the post-Communist societies in transition.

Nowadays, countries of Eastern Europe are actively preoccupied in remodeling their national criminal policies and legal systems in consonance with Western patterns. The collapse of an exclusivist ideology meant the end of a sole theory of punishment, which has been replaced by various approaches, often based on opposing but peacefully coexisting theses. Public opinion is similarly divided, swinging between excessive harshness, when calls for more severe penalties and retention of the death penalty, and generous leniency, which approaches in a moderate way the idea of criminal liability. Accordingly, law-makers seeking feasible Western models have created hybrid bodies of legislation, resulting from the wide variety of strategies adopted. A mature criminal policy, away from extremes, is a prerequisite to comprehensively reform the system of sanctions. A comparative analysis and an adequate selection of the Western criminal legislation products may offer an option not for a more intensive, but for a more varied system of penalties.

Part One: Alternatives to Custody surveys different trends in national criminal policies related to the treatment of offenders "outside" prison and "without" prison. Totalitarian regimes promoted a harsher sanctioning system, based on long-term imprisonment and strongly retributive substitutes; traditional societies, where the community plays a substantial role, have favored community-oriented sanctions, while the high-tech countries have developed such a sophisticated system of alternatives, that these do not function as substitutes for imprisonment, but rather as alternatives to each other.

Non-custodial alternatives are analyzed by group affiliations (pre-trial, sentencing and post-judicial substitutes; monetary penalties, community corrections) and system affiliation (civil law, common law, other legal systems).

Part Two: Probation Order is a thorough introspection of a highly employed community sentence in the common law countries and its growing impact on other legal systems. Probation did not have a distinct evolvement in the civil law countries, including the post-Communist ones, which favored instead suspended sentence with no supervision, but currently there is an interconnection between the two alternatives. From this perspective, we considered useful a contrastive analysis of their highs and lows, since each of them is very popular in the legal system they originated from.

The eternal conflict between the rehabilitative ideals and the *just desert* principles is pointed out in the analysis on the legal nature and the functions of probation. We attempted to detect a possible rationale for infusing probation to legal systems with no tradition in the field. For the same purposes, the evolution of probation was scrutinized both historically and in the long run. Its legal requirements (eligibility, granting conditions, breach, revocation, discharge, amendment, and rehabilitation) were examined in light of the current literature and caselaw. A brief criminological meta-analysis has quantified at the end "what works" and the success rates for different offender groups.

Part Three: Implementing Models examines the process of legal reform in the transitional societies. Currently, there are favorable conditions for implementing at least a part of the wide range of non-custodial programs employed in the United Kingdom and the United States, given the economic and financial availability of the recipient-states, their human resources and, to some extent, the spirit of the public. However, if used by a skilled staff, alternative sanctions can concomitantly satisfy rehabilitative ideals, offer a diversity of crime control strategies, and be cost-effective solutions for the post-Communist criminal justice systems.

THE AUTHOR
Washington, DC - August 1997

ACKNOWLEDGMENTS

My very warm and sincere thanks are due to the following:

- the University of Manchester, the London South Bank University and the Soros Foundation for an Open Society, joint sponsors for a Foreign and Commonwealth Office Scholarship which helped me finalize this study;
- the staff from the British Council (the Bucharest Office) who facilitated my access to the United Kingdom;
- the law librarians from the universities of Oxford (Bodleian) and Manchester (John Rylands), Greater Manchester Probation Service and NACRO Manchester, who actively assisted me in consulting the over 2,000 reference titles for this project, and especially to David Sparrow (Policy Support Unit, Greater Manchester Probation Service), Sue Bates (Law Librarian, John Rylands University Library), and Doreen Robinson (NACRO Manchester Documentary Office); also, to Robert Braun (Braun & Perez Law Offices, Philadelphia, USA), for providing part of the U.S. documentation;
- all the probation officers I interviewed and discussed with, who revealed many things not usually found in books, and especially to: Cedric Fullwood (Chief Probation Officer, Greater Manchester Probation Office), Robert Mathers, Susan Wildman, Maria Parker, Barbara Samson, Philip Lloyd (Greater Manchester Probation Service), Alec Shkandrij, Fran O'Deka (Salford Probation Office), Carol Morton, Frances Flaxington, Melva Burton (Manchester and Middleton probation offices, The Sex Offenders Division), Roger Tanner (NACRO Manchester), Hon. Mark Hammond, Dorothy Meredith, SPO (The Manchester Crown Court), Shirley Johnson, Pat Milnes (HM Prison Manchester), Francis Prittie, Paul Rogoff, Gordon Cutler, Tom Stanway (Probation Service Christian Fellowship), Lloyd La Rose-Jones (Association of Black Probation Officers, London), Muhammad Daullah

(National Association of Asian Probation Staff), Di Shipley (Lesbians and Gay Men in Probation Association, London), Susan Cawthra (Chair, Greater Manchester Probation Council), Mike Landriau (Chairman, Greater Manchester Victim Support Scheme);

- to the Home Office Probation Division and the Statistic Department, for useful discussions and valuable documentation, and especially to: Dr. George Mair (currently, at the Liverpool University), Prof. Mike Hough (currently, at the London South Bank University), Hugh Marriage, Gordon Barclay and the enthusiastic Sara Marshall (Home Office Special Conferences Unit, Liverpool);

Last, but not least, my high appreciation and gratitude go to Dr. Roger Hood (Director, Center for Criminological Research, University of Oxford), for his valuable advice, given in an early stage of my documentation, Thomas Gibbons (University of Manchester, Faculty of Law), who supervised this project in its final stage with competence and patience, and Aimée Stenzel, (American University, Washington DC), for her precious editorial assistance.

INTRODUCTION

A GLIMPSE FROM WEST TO EAST

At the end of century, we are witnessing historical structural changes on a worldwide level. The fall of communism in Eastern Europe in the late 1980s altered the social apparatus as maybe no other event since the two world wars has done. Its disappearance as a system meant not only the collapse of an ideology but a debut for national revival, with high impact on both the traumatized societies and individual mentalities. In order to shape an open society, the law had to adjust infrastructures and be, in turn, adjusted. The criminal justice system, as a social barometer, reflected to a great extent that evolution.

The countries which have been experiencing utopian ideals for over 40 years, and whose national penal systems were practicing organized repression and preaching a facade humanism, found themselves in front of a new beginning. How to resolve the multiple problems generated by a too long disruption between two parts of the same Europe? How long would the adjustment to the standards of a normal society take? Could there be a come back to the prewar type of democracy, a match on the fly to the Western models, or a search for genuine solutions? These were questions which penal reform could not be exempted from.

At a time when even Western democracies are changing their legislative models according to their ideology-makers, non-custodial sanctions in post-Communism remains an issue open to debate. What is unquestionable is the current need for models. Since reviving the old prewar democracy models might be obsolete nowadays, and jumping into the unknown could be risky enough, the bst solution at hand appears to be Western-model implementation, a feasible way in the long run.

Analyzing non-custodial sanctions is especially important for the former Communist countries, where freedom was, not long ago, perceived merely as an aspiration. Some of them, like limitation of certain rights, fine, suspended sentence and correctional labor were applied with some success against the first offenders, but used against some political dissidents, as well. Some others, such as exile or confiscation of assets, were criticized as obsolete even by the local scholars. Enforcing alternatives like correctional labor was always problematic for the Communist regimes. By law, supervision was entrusted to various company committees, whose members, representatives of the "working people," performed only formally their duties. Offender monitoring, a time-consuming job, was deemed as a burden for the normal functioning of the company. Beyond the Iron Curtain, the Western democracies were offering a completely different picture: a specialized supervision performed by high-skilled categories of professionals, namely social workers and probation officers. Communism created other anomalies, as well. While correctional labor was formally aimed to serve rehabilitation, it proved to be in fact vital for sustaining the national state-run economies. On the contrary, in the free-market world, convicts were employed for the type of activities otherwise performed by volunteers.

For those lawmakers favoring a treatment-oriented criminal justice system, non-custodial sanctions might offer new solutions against the growing mistrust for the rehabilitative function of custody, though the way of enforcing could visibly impact their evolution in the foreseeable future.

Finding feasible and implementable substitutes to imprisonment is a top priority for transitional post-Communist societies. Currently, there is an active preoccupation for remodeling the national penal policies and the legal systems in consonance with the Western patterns; also, for studying the effectiveness of various alternative models used in pre-trial, trial and post-detention process, especially of probation. Several factors generate such an interest: probation is by far the most popular sentence in the common law Western countries; it has an increasing impact on the related devices of the civil law system; last but not least, the East European statutory law, formerly of a collectivist tradition, where probation existed in a vestigial form only, is strongly oriented toward the Western patterns.

If political will can be properly attuned with the legislative efforts, the infusion of new legal devices would be a way for the societies in transition to access the circuit of the perennial democratic values.

PART ONE

ALTERNATIVES TO CUSTODY

CHAPTER 1

AN OVERVIEW

1.1. TRENDS IN CRIMINAL POLICIES

The subject of alternatives to imprisonment assumes a profound significance in light of the worldwide controversy concerning the role and functions of prison as an instrument of social control.[1] In the wake of rapid industrialization, urbanization and technological changes resulting in the erosion of the traditional social institutions, such as the family and the community, the prison appears to have been subjected to excessive use in most of developed and developing countries. Rising crime, prison overcrowding and the seeming inability of the criminal justice systems to cope effectively with the new patterns and dimensions of criminality have further accentuated the controversy on the use of imprisonment. Besides the classical arguments regarding the inherent contradictions between the custodial and the rehabilitative functions of prison, other factors such as the dehumanizing aspect of incarceration, the debilitating impact of a total institutionalization on the human personality, the increasing awareness that imprisonment is unlikely to improve the offender's chances of living a law-abiding life or to reduce the crime rate, have given a new impetus to the movement toward the treatment of offenders "outside" prison or "without" prison. While non-institutional forms of treatment have been widely recommended, the sanction of segregation from the community is still considered to be the strongest deterrent, both to individual offenders and to society at large, and imprisonment still appears to be necessary where the risk of repetition of a dangerous offense is high. In many countries of the world custody is deemed as the strongest deterrent, even for lesser crimes involving drugs. Others favor non-custodial sanctions, while caselaw of some countries indicate that alternatives have not been functioning as substitutes for imprisonment, but rather as alternatives to each other.

During the last two decades, most countries had to cope with significant increases of their prison population.[2] Therefore, a comparison between the general trend toward soaring prison populations and the development of policies favoring alternatives, like court supervision or non-custodial sentences, is worthwhile. Should the alternatives to prison be viewed as the sole solution for the persistent problem of prison overcrowding, they may be considered to be a failure. But the general picture changes if one looks beyond the growing number of inmates and analyzes instead the average length of detention, directly related with the duration of pre-trial and trial procedures and the amendments in legislation.[3] Also, in the last decade (1982-1991) the number of custodial sentences was in decrease; see **Table 1**.

No one can claim that the crime rate is, on general, decreasing in Europe, but one may assert that developing alternative policies for dealing with less serious crimes is not useless. Still, taking into account the longer periods of detention, they should not be seen as the only solution in resolving the problem of soaring prison population.

The above considerations make it clear that the question of alternatives to imprisonment must be analyzed within the broader context of the response of society to crime and in connection with the constraints under which the criminal justice system operates as a whole. Crime, as a social phenomenon, keeps on challenging humankind and still remains, as a form of human behavior, a subject of conceptual arguments and abstractions. In the absence of any wholly valid theory of crime causation, developing more appropriate methods of treatment for offenders remains a matter of theoretical debate. With a worldwide crime rate on the rise, scrutiny of how criminal justice works in terms of fairness and equity becomes more intense.[4]

Offender rehabilitation, a top priority in the 1960s and the 1970s, lost its credibility primarily because of the low ability of the therapy program promoters to eventually curb the crime rate. Thus, denunciations of prison and the calls for its total abolition have inevitably made the failure of the criminal justice system itself an easy scapegoat. The "therapeutic experiments" in the

Table 1:

Annual numbers of the custodial sentences in Europe (5-year averages)

COUNTRY	1982-86 =thousands=1987-91		TREND (%)
Romania	43.4	23.1	- 46.91
Italy	104.6	67.5	- 35.47
Greece	7.9	5.7	- 27.85
England & Wales	92.6	76.9	- 16.96
Belgium	21.2	17.9	- 15.57
Germany	107.7	93.6	- 13.10
Netherlands	24.7	22.5	- 8.91
Finland	9.7	9.0	- 7.22
Portugal	10.7	10.2	- 4.68
France	84.2	83.3	- 1.07
Ireland	6.8	7.2	+ 5.88
Spain	61.2	67.0	+ 9.47

Author's table. Sources:

European Sourcebook of Crime and Justice Statistics, Strasbourg, European Committee on Crime Problems (CDPC), 1995;

Romanian Statistical Yearbook 1993, Bucharest, National Commission for Statistics (CNS), 1994.

1970s have proved it in excess. The loss of confidence in the offender's treatment and rehabilitation of offenders led, first in the United States and then in Europe, to the revisiting of the neoclassical retributive principles. In the late 1970s and the 1980s, criminal experts started to question the role of correction in the justice process, the relative balance between punishment and treatment as correctional objectives, and the effectiveness of many correctional programs and practices enforced at the time. They reexamined the basic philosophical assumptions about the functions of custody in a system of crime control. They also explored, assessed and applied some novel measures and policies in the field.[5]

Moreover, they evaluated the rationale, the consequences and the feasibility of the "treatment" ideology.[6] Nonetheless, during the following decade the "nothing works" slogan itself was equally criticized, and the sentencing process was severely scrutinized as to its fairness and capacity to lessen unwarranted disparities.[7] At the same time, the rising level of expectations among the underprivileged members of society produced intensive pressure for condition improvement in penitentiaries, and the emphasis placed upon the importance of human rights for prisoners contributed in bringing prison conditions to the forefront of public debate. In the 1990s, a much more individualized society was to focus on the victim's rights and the offender's responsibility.[8] Even so, due to the low efficiency of some retributive models, a reexamination of the non-custodial alternatives appears useful.

1.2. THE NEED FOR ALTERNATIVE MEASURES

Starting with the 1970s, most national lawmakers, in order to further humanize the correctional process, brought important innovations to their sanctioning systems. The amended legislations were usually dealing with a wider range of alternatives to imprisonment. In many countries, asset- and income-based fines began to surpass 90% of the court sentences. Restitution and victim compensation schemes started to be extensively used, while probation, suspended sentences, community service orders and other alternatives were contributing to reduce imprisonment rates, especially for first offenders. Cross-cultural research suggested that the length of imprisonment is either unrelated to recidivism, or it can even provoke it. While there have been operated reductions in the length of prison sentences in favor of medium and short-term sentences, no adverse effects on the deterrent value of imprisonment have been noticed.

Demands for an intensive employment of alternative measures and a more humane use of imprisonment, are based not only on the general requisites of humanity, justice and tolerance, but also on the interpretation of official crime data and various research findings. This experience may be summarized as follows: there is a lack of concordance between the prison institution as a "means" and the rehabilitation of offenders as a "goal" of sentencing. Prison tends to further criminalize a convicted offender and, in terms of any cost-benefit analysis, imprisonment is costly as to human and social resources. Any action, social or legal, is presumably inadequate if it cannot achieve its desired objective, and it is dysfunctional if it has the opposite effect. A custodial sentence is a socio-legal action aimed at achieving one, or a combination of, the following purposes: *retribution* ("just deserts"), *deterrence* (general and individual prevention), *incapacitation* (social defense and protection of individuals), and *correction* (reformation or rehabilitation).[9] However, its "essential" aim, recognized and accepted by the community of nations, is offender resocialization leading to a law-abiding and a self-supporting life, as stated in the *Standard Minimum Rules for the Treatment of Prisoners* (Rule 56) and in the *International Covenant on Civil and Political Rights* (Art. 10).

Non-custodial devices emerged and developed long before incarceration, but even afterwards they were viewed as alternatives for the low capacity of prisons to concomitantly absorb and resocialize offenders.

The traditional non-institutional responses to crime are still parcel of many indigenous penal systems and, in the context of indigenous social control, they appear to be efficient (e.g. various forms of restitution and reparation). While in the past they were sporadically experimented with by charitable organizations, nowadays they are part of the global penal strategies.[10]

Governmental efforts and resources are being increasingly devoted to the development of new, or the redevelopment of old alternatives, as a remedy for the shortcomings of the process of rehabilitation in prison and the deinstitutionalization of the therapeutic devices. In fact, society has not

Table 2:*The custodial sanctions and the alternatives to custody*

Stage Sanctions	PRE-TRIAL (police/prosecutor)	SENTENCING (courts)	POST-JUDICIAL (corrections)
Custodial	-arrest; remand; -pre-trial detention;	-conviction;	-prison;
Non- custodial	-decriminalization; -diversion programs; -police; -deferred/suspended prosecution; -bail; -release on recognizance supervision; -half-way house; -community center;	-admonition; -reprimand; -restitution; - disqualification/ deprivation of certain rights; /-fine; day-fine; -confiscation; -expropriation; -compensation; -conditional or absolute discharge; -suspended or conditional sentence; -probation; -judicial supervision; -restriction of liberty; -correctional labor; -community service order; -community attendance centers; -weekend imprisonment; -semi-open detention; -special health treatment; -amnesty; pardon;	-furlough; -license on -recognizance; -work or educational and conditional release -partly suspended sentences; -community programs; -half-way house; -parole; -amnesty; -pardon;

Author's table. Source: UN Secretariat, *Alternatives to Imprisonment*, ST/ESA/SER.M/36, New York, 1983.

removed all the mentally disturbed and the retarded to asylums, nor has it sent the poor or the elderly to workhouses. Care and support for such people went back to community. By reverting these responsibilities to the community and by supplying adequate means for these purposes, the society may lower the feeling of powerlessness and fragmentation of some of its members.

Deinstitutionalization can be undertaken at all levels of the criminal justice system: at the pre-trial stage, that is the police and prosecutorial level; upon conviction, as a judicial disposition; and after the imposition of a prison sentence, usually as a result of an evaluation by the correctional authorities; see **Table 2**.[11]

CHAPTER 2

THE CIVIL LAW SYSTEM

2.1. WESTERN EUROPE

A global classification of the non-custodial sanctions, despite some inherent limits imposed by local historical diversity and legal specificity, outlines two basic categories:

(a) alternatives consisting in executing the custodial sanction by reducing the possibility of incarceration either quantitatively (*house arrest, curfew orders, weekend imprisonment, semi-detention*) or qualitatively (*semi-liberty*), tolerating contact with external milieu and avoiding the disruption of daily life activities;

(b) alternatives involving judicial suspension of punishment, generally escorted by special conditions, accepted by the convict, characterized by the activity of supervision carried on by specialized staff. In a large range, from the classic *suspended sentence* and *probation,* including their combined variants, to *parole,* these alternatives are widely used in the Western European countries.

Monetary penalties (*fine, day-fine*) and **economic sanctions**, either accessories to detention (*confiscation*) or autonomous ones (*bail* under different forms), are frequently used against petty criminals. In special cases, monetary penalties can be converted into incarceration or other measures (when fine is not paid), or be themselves the result of custodial conversions (for short-term imprisonment); the upper limit varies from 1-month (Italy, Law 689 of 1981) to 3-month (the Netherlands, Art. 24 of the Penal Code) or 6-month imprisonment (Austria, Art. 37 of the Penal Code). These alternatives as such may constitute conditions for different types of probation or supervision, in case of restitution or victim compensation.

Day-fine system has been operating in Austria, Denmark, Germany and Sweden, by multiplying a certain figure, which takes into account the seriousness of the offense and the dangerousness of the offender, with an amount of money fitting the convict's financial possibilities. In some countries, the day-fine has become an attractive alternative for short-term imprisonment, usually for up to 6-months (Germany, France, the Scandinavian countries, Portugal).

Periodic detention, though with no repercussions upon the position of the convict, is the micro-version of classical custody. It can take the form of a *home confinement* or other form of deprivation of liberty at large. In Italy, home confinement during remand is provided for drug addicts (Law 532 of 1982).

Weekend imprisonment, as an autonomous penalty, has been initiated in Belgium (by Ordinance of 15 February 1963), and adopted later on in Germany (for juveniles, *Jugendarrest*), Switzerland and Turkey; it consists of serving a certain amount of hours in prison, computed from the length of detention.[1]

Semi-liberty, granted for short convictions (up to 3-months or 6-months imprisonment), requires a certain amount of hours served in custody (Belgium), or serving the sentence after hours (Italy, 1975; Portugal, Art. 45 of Decree-Law 400 of 1982), and imposes certain responsibilities for the offender aimed at his social rehabilitation.

Periodic penalty reduction system, practiced in Italy, consists of substituting a 5-day period in prison with a 6-month period of good behavior. Technically, this is not a pure substitute but rather a device to reduce detention.[2]

Suspended sentence is an alternative frequently applied by courts. In Germany, Switzerland and Spain, it is applicable *ex officio* once the required conditons are fulfilled. In Portugal, it is commonly employed by the juvenile courts.[3] Caselaw research on suspended sentence is hindered by some inadequate criminological research and statistics, whose shortcomings have often been pointed out. On two essential points, information is extremely poor: the influence of the personality of offenders on the use of suspended sentence and the effectiveness of the method.

In France, the use of suspended sentence or the *sursis simple* (adopted in 1891) has been sensibly influenced by factors related to the type of jurisdiction, penalty, offense, personality of offenders, and, since 1958, by a version of statutory probation or the *sursis avec mise a l'epreuve* (Art. 738 of the Code of Penal Procedure).

Due to its satisfactory results in preventing recidivism, suspended sentence keeps its high rate of applicability in court despite the emergence of some new alternatives having more flexible conditions for granting. In Italy, it passes well over 40%, and in France, Germany and Finland it ranges between 30-40%. Yet, other countries, like Greece, have rates below 15%. [4]

Probation consists in the conditional suspension of the execution of penalty, plus some additional conditions related to the supervision of the offender performed by a specialized staff. France was the first civil law country that promoted probation (by the 1884 Berenger bill), and Belgium the first one which enforced it (by the 1888 Lejeune Act). Then, it was taken over in various versions by the other national legislations: first, in France (the 1891 Berenger Act), then in Luxembourg and Switzerland (1892), Portugal, (1893), Italy (1904), Denmark (1905), Sweden (1906), Spain (1908), the Netherlands (1915), Norway (1919), Austria (1920). Initially, those eligible for probation were first offenders and 6-month convicts,[5] then 5-year convicts (e.g., in Denmark). The supervision component was statutorily provided much later, beginning in the 1960s (France, 1958, 1970, 1975, 1981; Denmark, 1961; Belgium, 1964; Luxembourg, 1973; Italy, 1975).

In time, elements of Anglo-American probation were incorporated into the Franco-Belgian civil law system, such as the adjournment in pronouncing the sentence and the imposition of certain conditions to the offender. Thus, countries like Finland, France, Italy, Germany, Portugal, Luxembourg and the Netherlands have created their own combined forms of suspended sentence, probation, and imprisonment.[6]

Community service, a native institution of England and Wales, has been revigorated lately by the Continental statutory law. In Italy, *substitutive labor* does not replace imprisonment, but a fine only (Law 689 of 1981). In Germany and Portugal, it may replace up to 3-month imprisonment, under the supervision of social workers. In France, it is an unpaid activity in the benefit of the community, for a 10-month period (40 to 240 hours), and may be an imprisonment substitute (*le travail d'interet general*) or a special suspended sentence (imposing the condition of carrying out the "labor of general interest").

Parole (release on license), a post-judicial alternative, is the conditional release of an inmate, usually after he has served one-half of the sentence for less serious crimes, and two-thirds for more serious ones, and upon certain conditions. Unlike suspended sentence or probation, it is aimed rehabilitating offenders serving longer term imprisonment. As an institution of English inspiration, it was implemented for the first time in Belgium (1883) and France (1885), as an alternative for adults, then taken over by Italy (1889), Portugal (1893), Sweden (1906), Norway (1911) and Denmark (1920).

The release is granted by either the Ministry of Justice or the governor of the prison. If a parolee committed an offense during the period of his original sentence, he may have to serve any part of the original sentence still outstanding. In such cases, his right to be reconsidered for parole will be subject to limitation. Statutory laws in Spain, Switzerland, the Netherlands, and Luxembourg provided similar regulations.

2.2. EASTERN EUROPE

While theorists in the former Communist bloc were asserting a natural evolution of non-custodial sanctions in the system, the Communist regimes were constantly concerned with effectiveness of incarceration,[7] especially for crimes against state property. Criminal statutes of those countries were influenced both by Soviet Russia and by international law instruments. Usually, non-custodial alternatives were matching one of two categories, namely:

(a) the so-called "traditional" alternatives: *monetary penalties* and other *economic sanctions, restrictions of the right to free movement, deprivation of certain rights, admonition, suspended sentence*;

(b) work-based alternatives, served in an open milieu: *correctional labor*.

Traditional alternatives survived Communism and they currently coexist with some new implemented alternatives of Western inspiration, such as bail, bail on supervision, suspended sentence with supervision, and probation, which are to be analyzed thereafter.

Punishment by **fine** is almost similar, although not identical, in all the East European countries. As a rule, a fine may be passed either as a sanction on its own merits (for minor offenses) or in combination with other sanctions, usually imprisonment (for more serious offenses). In Poland,[8] and Hungary,[9] as a complementary sanction, fine has larger limits than as a separate sanction. In Yugoslavia, the former is applicable to offenders who attempt to obtain illegal benefits or cause damage to public property. In the Czech Republic, courts do not fine insolvent offenders. Usually, lawmakers tend to restrain the court discretionary power by setting statutory limits for fines. Yet the Penal Code in Bulgaria fixed the minimum limit only, while in Russia there is no statutory limit. In Hungary, whose legislation was more open to the Western influence, the 1978 Penal Code adopted a day-fine system (10 to 180 days and up to 270 days for concurrent offenses), where the amount per day is fixed according with the offender's financial capabilities.

Confiscation, an accessory penalty to capital punishment or imprisonment, used frequently by the Communist regimes, consisted in compulsory transfer to state ownership, with no compensation, of all or part of the convict's property and applied to crimes against the "socialist property."

In post-Communism, constitutionality of confiscation has been questioned often, since "socialist property" became a superfluous concept. In Hungary, mandatory forfeiture of property has been abolished, unless illegal profits were made by committing a criminal act.[10] In 1993, the Constitutional Court in Romania held that providing a different penal regime for offenses against property, depending on its public or private nature (i.e., higher limits of sanctioning plus confiscation for offenses against public, former "socialist," property), is unconstitutional, and therefore, the Penal Code regulations making such a distinction must be deemed as repealed (Decision no. 1 of September 7, 1993). This viewpoint is not yet unanimously accepted by the East European scholars.[11] In Russia, confiscation has been used quite frequently, even in the 1990s (10% of the total sanctions).[12]

Another typical non-custodial sanction, adopted in the early years of Communism, was **expropriation**, designed and applied against political opponents. In the Czech Republic, the new democratic regime passed in 1989 a decree returning all nationalized assets to the former landlords. In Romania, the 1996 elected government has taken similar steps.[13]

Limitation to free movement consists in either obligation to reside in specified areas (e.g., exile of 2 to 5 years, regulated by Art. 25 of the former Soviet Union Penal Code and Art. 69 of the Russian Code of Correctional Labor), or prohibition to reside in certain localities (e.g., banishment, in Russia and other former Soviet republics, Bulgaria, and Romania, provided by Art. 112(d) of the Romanian Penal Code), or expulsion from the national territory, applied to aliens (a sanction *per se* in former East Germany, former Czechoslovakia, and Hungary, a preventive measure in former Yugoslavia and Romania). Exile and banishment were strongly criticized as being ineffective and too expensive, even during the communist period.

Deprivation of certain rights was applicable to certain professionals (e.g., doctors who performed illegal abortions, in Russia and Romania), high officials committing certain types of offenses, and individuals making illegal profits from unskillful activities (in Bulgaria). There were some legislative attempts to use them as alternatives for short-term imprisonment and correctional labor.

Admonition (reprimand) has been seldom used (1%) in Bulgaria, Russia,[14] and Romania (for minors); court decisions are occasionally published by local press, or posted at the offender's workplace.

Suspended sentence (conditional suspension of the execution of penalty) has early precedents in Eastern Europe (Hungary, 1908; Romania, 1920, after prior initiatives in 1897).[15] Designed as an alternative for short-term incarceration (up to 2 years for intentional offenses, in Czech Republic; 3 years for offenses committed by negligence, in Poland,[16] Bulgaria, Romania and Yugoslavia), it prescribes a set of requirements for the convict, and does not usually apply to repeat offenders (in Bulgaria, Hungary, Poland and Romania). The Penal Code in Romania introduced both suspended sentence (Art. 81) and conditional sentence, that is suspended sentence with supervision (Art. 86/1-6). Probation period ranges from 2 to 5 years, and it usually includes a term equal with the duration of the sentence (set by court) plus a fixed term (set by legislator).

In the 1970s, Russia adopted a combined version of suspended sentence with correctional labor. In the 1980s, in some countries suspended sentence was about 20-50% of the total number of sanctions (50% in Yugoslavia, 30-45% in Poland,[17] 28-35% in Bulgaria, former Czechoslovakia, 20-25% in Hungary), while in others it never ran over 15% (6-17% in the 1950s and the 1960s and 11-14% in the 1990s, in Russia,[18] 4.5% in the 1980s, in Romania).[19]

Probation did not have an autonomous existence until legal reform in the past years, when the Western models have been more or less assimilated, and have survived in a vestigial form in Hungary and the Czech Republic. Hungary has a specialized staff for supervision and its current legislation allows repeat offenders to be placed on probation. In Romania, the 1968 Penal Code provided for a kind of probation for minors, called *supervised liberty*. Much later, the Law 104 of 1992 adopted conditional sentence, called "suspension of the execution of penalty on supervision" and prefigured the role of probation officers. A 1997 probation draft law has outlined post-conviction rehabilitation in progressive stages.[20] Nonetheless, setting up a national probation service remains a task difficult to accomplish due to the economic hardships of transition.

Correctional labor was by far the most popular non-custodial alternative in the Eastern European bloc. Adopted by the former Soviet Union after the 1917 October Revolution, it was copied, with some variations, by the rest of the countries in the Soviet bloc. Originally, it merely consisted of compulsory hard labor, served at the offender's workplace and partly remunerated. The Soviet model was followed closely by Bulgaria and Poland. In Poland, the 1969 Penal Code set forth a lenient version, called *limitation of liberty*, consisting of unpaid supervised work for the community of 20 to 50 hours per month for a 3-month to 2-year period. In Romania, Decree 218 of 1977 (now repealed) imposed on the courts to apply correctional labor instead of up to 5 years custody, triggering a spectacular drop in the incarceration rate (from 66% in 1976 to 29.4% in 1979) and an artificial drop of crime rate.[21] Russia frequently used correctional labor, both in the Soviet era and post-Communist period (20-25% in the 1970s, 18-20% in the 1990s).[22] But in general, implementation of free-market machinery made the enforcement of correctional labor a difficult task both in Russia and other East European countries (e.g., in Romania it dropped from 37% in the 1980s, to 18% in the

1990s)[23] and, in some cases, even an impossible one (in Hungary, "strict" correctional work was abolished).[24]

2.3. LATIN AMERICA

By tradition, Latin American statutes employed the European patterns, where classical sanctions coexisted with security measures, of positivist inspiration. As a result, the long-lasting ideological conflict between the "just desert" principles and therapeutic models developed a certain eclecticism in the penal treatment of offenders.

Security measures were adopted in the 1930s (Cuba, 1936), but their therapeutic essence has been diluted by statutes.[25] Doctrinally, they were adopted as a result of liberal policies supporting the treatment-over-punishment positivist ideology, but substantially they were not so different from custody (e.g., the "preventive" acts against vagrancy, deriving from Spanish law), the main distinction consisting in the dangerousness threshold of offense, otherwise very flexible. Precarious economic situations in many Latin American countries prevented the creation of national networks of supervisors, which made security measures less effective than classical alternatives.

Other alternatives (e.g., *fine, confiscation, deprivation of certain rights*), followed the classical concept of a punishment scale, rather than being used as substitutes to custody.

Probation and *parole* are both products of the above mentioned eclectic approach in sanctioning. Legally, they derive from custodial sanctions, although substantively they are non-custodial measures of security.

Suspended sentence, in both the standard form and its version with supervision, followed the French model of the *sursis simple* and the *sursis avec mise a l'epreuve*. The latter was favored by lawmakers in Argentina (enacted in 1906, and enforced in 1921),[26] Brazil (1924),[27] and Chile (1944).[28] In spite of some legislative initiatives, suspended sentence with supervision turned itself ultimately into the standard suspended sentence, due to precarious human and financial resources.

Probation is usually granted to first offenders whose conviction is lower than 2-years imprisonment (Argentina, Colombia) or 3-years imprisonment

(Costa Rica). National probation boards were established in Argentina, Brazil, Mexico and Uruguay (in the late 1960s), Honduras (1976), Venezuela (1980) and Costa Rica (1981).[29]

Parole is granted frequently in some countries (20% of the convicts, in Peru), while others have lower rates (Costa Rica). Argentina and Venezuela have used parole boards since 1918, while in other countries parole networks are in progress.

CHAPTER 3

THE COMMON LAW SYSTEM

3.1. UNITED KINGDOM

Pre-trial alternatives, also known as *diversion programs* or *diversionary devices*, are procedures that suspend the criminal proceedings provided the offender accepts guidance or treatment from specialized agencies. Some of these alternatives are employed by the judicial authorities as part of their discretionary prerogatives or may be dependent on the availability of the rehabilitation centers (e.g., the drug treatment centers). Others do not require use of institutionalized facilities (e.g., summonses, citations, bail and release on recognizance or with supervision).

Bail is a deposit paid by somebody temporarily released from custody in order to guarantee his return to stand trial. It is disposed by a magistrates' court or the Crown Court.[1] **Release on recognizance** or **on supervision** requires the offender to report periodically to his supervisor, who maintains a minimum level of assistance.

Initially, bail implied a "recognizance," that is an acknowledgment of a debt to the Queen, payable on default of compliance with a set of required conditions. *The Bail Act 1976* abolished personal recognizance but preserved it for sureties. *The Bail (Amendment) Act 1993*, enforced in 1994, empowered Crown Prosecutors to apply to a Crown Court judge for reassessing the bail decision when bail is granted by a magistrates' court to someone charged with or convicted of an offense punishable with a term of imprisonment of 5 years or more; and *The Criminal Justice and Public Order Act 1994* empowered police custody officers to grant conditional bail to people who have been charged, on the same basis and criteria as courts can impose conditions of bail, with certain exceptions. Services offering bail support to defendants who might otherwise be denied bail in criminal courts have been in operation in some local authority and probation areas of England and Wales for a number of years; e.g., the Nottinghamshire Bail Support Scheme for young people, applied since 1983.[2]

The range of **sentencing alternatives** is wide and deserves a certain categorization. Broadly, there are *compensation and restitution, discharges and bind-overs, monetary or financial penalties, suspended sentences* and *community sentences.*

(a) **Compensation** and **restitution** are remedies for offenses against persons and property. A compensation order can be made independently for a particular offense or in addition to any other sentence or order. Courts are required to regard the means of the offender when deciding whether to make a compensation order and when deciding on its amount. The magistrates' court can order compensations not exceeding £5,000 per offense, while the Crown Court can make such orders irrespective of the amount.

Victim compensation can also be carried out by the probation service and some private organizations, through so-called *mediation schemes* or *projects.* Mediation is based on two basic elements: a conciliatory meeting between the offender and his victim, organized by a social worker or probation officer, and some form of restitution or compensation. In 1990, England employed 31 such "mediation schemes" out of which 17 were specially designed to settle disputes between neighbors. Their effectiveness has been assessed as promising.[3]

(b) A court may **discharge** a convicted person either absolutely or conditionally, when the court takes the view that it is not necessary to impose punishment. According to *The Criminal Justice Act 1991,* s. 29, as amended in 1993 and 1994, discharge now counts as a *conviction.* An *absolute discharge* requires nothing from the offender and imposes no restrictions on future conduct. Most discharges are *conditional,* where criminal liability for the original offense is preserved in case of reoffending within a maximum period of 3 years.

A **binding-over order** relates, to a certain extent, to a suspended fine. It is used more in the way of preventive justice, for it allows the magistrates to warn citizens as to their future good conduct (e.g., binding over to keep the peace). If the person fails to keep the peace or exhibit good behavior during a stated period (up to 12 months) he may forfeit a sum of money (*recognizance*); if the person does not agree to being bound over, he can be sent to prison for up to 6 months. Binding-over orders are often used in inter-neighbor disputes, poison-pen writers, and *mala fide* suitors. There is a danger that magistrates might misuse their wide powers (over 8,000 orders per year are made under *The Justice of the Peace Act 1361* and *The Magistrates' Courts Act 1980*). Civil-liberty groups have often complained that demonstrators and protesters have been bound over for no good reason and that, in effect, the powers have been used to take away the right of free speech and protest.[4] Some courts found bind-overs unnecessary and theorists suggested on their abolition due to their inconsistency and unfairness.[5]

(c) In practice, the **fine** is by far the most important form of sentence (80% of magistrates' court sentences). The means of an offender may affect the amount of a fine, but it should not influence the basic decision of whether or not to fine him. Sometimes a fine supervision order will be made, which requires the offender to be placed under the care of a probation officer, who can encourage him to work out his financial problems so that he can then pay off the installments. But, if all else fails, the offender who does not pay his fine can be sent to prison.

The fine should be carefully related to the means of the offender, otherwise he will be committed to prison in default and there will be no advantage. Evidence suggests that fine defaulters believe the class differences between themselves and the magistracy are an important reason why the rate of payments is set at too high a level. Yet the idea of using economic incentives to minimize the rate of fine default (e.g., by offering discounts for prompt payment) was not actively supported by the government.[6]

The day-fine system has been introduced in England quite recently and on an experimental basis. The advantage of day-fine is that the punishment element of it can certainly be as harsh as that of a prison sentence. Furthermore, some offenders see a heavy fine as a harsher punishment than a prison sentence.

All offenses warranting a fine, except serious violent crimes and sex offenses, are ranked according to their gravity and then converted into a number of day-fines or fine-units; the weekly income is calculated after making allowances for fixed expenses and costs incurred for the number of dependents, after which the fixed percentage of the weekly income is multiplied by the number of fine-units.[7]

(d) A court is empowered to order, in certain circumstances, a **suspended sentence** when a person is sentenced to imprisonment for less than 2 years under the condition that he shall not commit another offense within a specified operational period of between 1 and 2 years.

If the suspended sentence is for a prison term exceeding 6 months, the court may also make a *suspended sentence supervision order*, placing the offender under the care of a probation officer (in case of breach, he is liable to a fine). The idea of introducing the suspended sentence, as a more effective deterrent against breaching the probation orders, was launched in 1950 by Sir Leo Page. The police backed up the proposal, considering suspended sentence to be more acceptable to courts and to the public in serious cases than a conditional discharge, and more effective on the offender. This question was considered in detail by the Home Office Advisory Council in 1951, but at that time the idea of suspended sentence was considered "wrong in principle and to a large extent impracticable" and, accordingly, no further recommendation had been made.[8] When suspended sentence was first introduced in 1967, courts were obliged by statute (until 1972) to suspend almost all prison sentences of 6 months or less. In practice, a series of malfunctions were identified: tendency of courts to impose suspended sentences on some occasions when immediate custody could not be justified (reducing initially the prison population, a phenomenon counterbalanced afterwards by the increasing number of activated sentences as a result of breaches); tendency to impose longer sentences when suspending than when imposing an immediate prison sentence (noticeable at magistrates' courts); and, finally, suspension made in appropriate cases (e.g., for theft in breach of trust). In practice, many offenders view suspended sentence as a "let off"[9] since it places no restrictions other than the obligation not to offend again. As a result, *The Criminal Justice Act 1991* (s. 5) further restricted the suspended sentence of imprisonment to cases in which immediate custody would have been justified (as in the previous statute), and if there are "exceptional circumstances" which justify its suspension; it also requires the court to consider whether it would be appropriate to impose a fine or make a compensation order at the same time. As for "exceptional circumstances," should the interpretation of the term have been more rigorous, they would not have created abundant caselaw.[10] Yet the courts have shown great flexibility when dealing with such circumstances; e.g., in the *Ullah Khan* case,[11] a fraudulent solicitor's serious health problems were considered sufficiently exceptional. Despite all these, the appeal rate against suspended sentence was low (2% in 1992).[12]

(e) **Community sentences** are applicable for offenses with an intermediate degree of seriousness, requiring something less than custody but more than a bind-over or a discharge. They include one or more community orders, which, in turn, can be mixed with other measures, such as fines and compensation. In time, community orders have become a diverse group, since in the past century they were adopted by statutes at different legislative moments, against a changing penological background dealing concomitently with rehabilitative ideals and the principles of punishment in the community. *The CJA 1991* increased and strengthened the range of punishments available in the community. They are now regarded as penalties in their own right, not as alternatives to the execution of a custodial sentence. The main options are: *attendance center orders, supervision orders, probation orders, community service orders, combination orders,* and *curfew orders.* The court must weigh the degree of restriction of liberty that the order involves against the seriousness of the offense, and take account of the suitability of the order for the offender.

(e.1) An **attendance center order** is applicable to offenders aged 10 to 20 years old and enforced by junior or senior centers. Prior to *The Criminal Justice Act 1982*, which abolished Borstal training, the power to make these orders was confined to magistrates' courts. It now may be made by the Crown Court, an adult magistrates' court or a juvenile court, requiring attendance at a specified center for a certain number of hours. Since it is a community order, the court can impose an attendance center order if the conditions relating to the passing of a community order are satisfied; e.g., *CJA 1991*, s. 6 asks the court to be satisfied that the offense committed is serious enough to warrant a community order. The period of attendance ordered by the court (less than 12 hours for offenders under 14, between 12-24 hours for those under 17, and between 24-36 hours for those of 17 or over) is normally divided into 2-hour sessions, including physical training or tasks under supervision such as cleaning and upkeep of the premises. The aim is to maintain firm discipline throughout the period of attendance and to educate the youths in a proper use of leisure.[13]

The attendance centers were initiated and financed by the Home Office who asked the police authorities to set up such centers in their jurisdiction. This initiative was not very successful, though. Between 1981 and 1991 the proportionate use made by the courts of attendance center orders when sentencing for indictable offenses declined steadily (drop from 3% to 2%, i.e. from 14,000 to 5,700 offenders), and in 1987 there were only 24 centers left in all England. The initial objective, to provide an alternative sentence for 17-20 year-old-offenders is now under question mark. In practice, courts often use this prerogative when dealing with football hooligans, ordering for attendance on Saturday afternoons.

(e.2) **Supervision orders** are broadly equivalent to probation orders but supplied for younger offenders.[14] A supervision order may be passed by the Crown Court or a juvenile court (but not an adult magistrates' court) on 10-17 year-old offenders. *The CJA 1991* has lowered the age range for probation orders, by including the offenders aged 16. Accordingly, now there is a significant overlap between probation orders and supervision orders for offenders aged 16 and 17. While both a supervision order and a probation order are intended to assist an offender to become more responsible and to keep out of trouble, the clearest distinguishing feature is that the supervision order is also intended to help a young person to develop into an adult, whereas a probation order is more appropriate for someone who is already emotionally, intellectually, socially and physically an adult.[15] Supervision orders are designed to provide a demanding but constructing sentencing option for young people.[16] A supervision order is a "community order" and the court will not be able to impose a supervision order unless the conditions relating to the passing of a community order are satisfied.

The Crown Court can issue supervision orders, unless it considers as more desirable to remit the offender to a juvenile court instead. The juvenile court is the place where most of the orders are made. A supervision order will last for 3 years from the date on which it was made, or for such shorter period as may be specified in the order (there is no minimum period), but in practice supervision orders are usually made for 1 year or 2 years. The order places the juvenile under the supervision of either a social worker belonging to the local authority or a probation officer. In the latter case, the supervisor will be one of those working in the petty sessions area where the juvenile lives, and his duty is "to advise, assist and befriend the supervised person;" *The Children and Young Persons Act 1969*, s. 14. Usually, young offenders attend full-time discussion groups and taped sessions with local community members and youth workers. Meetings on a weekly basis, with 2-hour afternoon sessions (between 5.00 and 7.00 p.m.), and pick-up services supplied (ensuring that a minimum amount of time is spent out and about on the streets) appears to be highly effective.[17]

The court has the power to include any other requirement deemed, such as: residence, intermediate treatment, curfews, treatment for a mental condition, drug or alcohol dependency.

(e.3) **Probation order** applies to offenders aged 16 or over and requires a 6-month to 3-year probation service supervision. *The CJA 1991* upgraded probation from a non-custodial alternative ("instead of sentencing") to a punishment (sentence in its own right). The court may not impose a community sentence, consisting of one or more community orders, unless the offense was "serious enough to warrant such a sentence;" *CJA 1991*, s. 6(1). In practice, the court must be satisfied that the offense was too serious for a mere fine or discharge, with or without a compensation order. If the court so decides, then the community order(s) it makes must be the most suitable for the offender, and impose only such restrictions on liberty as are commensurate with the seriousness of the offense. A probation order may be made by the Crown Court, by an adult magistrates' court or by a juvenile court. The offender must consent to the making of the order.

A court may make a probation order in the interests of securing the rehabilitation of the offender, protecting the public from harm from him, or preventing the commission of further offenses.[19] The supervision is carried out by a designated probation officer who is responsible to the court for the planning, coordination and delivery of the supervision program, but the court has the power to include any other requirement considered appropriate. This could include residence, activities, attendance at a probation center, and treatment for a mental condition, drug or alcohol dependency. *The Powers of Criminal Courts Act 1973*, as amended by *The CJA 1991*, provided a large set of requirements related to accommodation and activities, which may be attached to the order.

In certain areas, probation centers run up to 60-day core courses, as a probation order requirement.[20]

In the past decade, probation orders increased constantly for all main categories of offenses (3%, on average), though their use in court may be limited by future legislation.

A more detailed approach is made in **Part Two**, which deals exclusively with probation order.

(e.4) **Community service orders** were introduced by *The Criminal Justice Act 1972*, largely as a result of the recommendations from the Advisory Council of the Penal System, in order to reduce the prison population. The relevant powers of the courts to pass community service orders are now to be found in *The PCCA 1973* (s. 14), as amended by *The CJA 1991* (s. 10).[21] Prior to 1991, the legal guidelines on the status of community service and custody were ambiguous and fueled doctrinal controversies.[22] *The PCCA 1973* defined community service as an order relevant to offenses which are "punishable with imprisonment," leaving open to interpretation whether community service order actually replaces a custodial sentence, another alternative to custody or a non-custodial penal measure. As a result, the order has been used in practice either as a sentence in its own right, an alternative to custody, or an alternative to probation and fines. Moreover, the idea that community service should not be used exclusively as a non-custodial alternative got support in courts and probation services since its inception. Whereas the English application stems from a "tariff system" (sentence as payment for crime), in practice, community service used to be ordered for offenses that vary greatly in seriousness, blurring its position in the tariff system.[23] *The CJA 1991* settled the issue in clearer terms. Community service was no longer presented as an alternative to custody, but as a demanding form of punishment in the community instead. Presumably, the order was designed for those who commit moderately serious offenses, much too serious to warrant a mere fine but insufficiently serious for custody. Some probation areas use "risk of custody" scales, in order to assess which cases are likely to be serious enough for community service.

A community service order may be made on an offender aged 16 years or over and requires the person to perform unpaid work of 40 to 240 hours duration. There is no upper age limit, but in practice this measure applies frequently to offenders in their late teens or twenties (over 35,000 orders per year). Certain categories of offenders are not eligible, e.g., the mentally disturbed, alcoholics, drug-addicts, the homeless. The hours set by the court should be completed within 1 year of the making of the order; however, the order remains in force until the hours are completed. According to the Home Office *National Standards*, the main purpose of such an order is to prevent further offending by reintegrating the offender into the community through punishment (by means of positive and demanding unpaid work, keeping to disciplined requirements) and reparation for the community (by undertaking socially useful work).[24] Work for offenders is found with local voluntary or public bodies or on projects directly organized by the probation service. All work, unpaid and normally undertaken by voluntary effort, falls into two broad categories: tasks of a practical nature not involving personal relationships with individuals, and those involving some contact with the beneficiaries. Examples of the sort of work done include painting and decorating houses and flats for the elderly and handicapped, taking part in archaeological excavations, repairing toys for children in need, building adventure playgrounds, doing site clearance work, helping in outdoor conservation projects, or other tasks ordered by the court.[25] Personal tasks include coaching swimming for handicapped children, visiting and helping the elderly and hospital patients, and helping at disabled people's sports clubs. So far as practicable the offender is given a task which will not conflict with his normal work or educational commitments or his religious beliefs. It is not unusual for an offender to become so involved in his task that he continues with it after fulfilling the terms of his order. The element of reparation involved in community service is symbolic, since it does not involve direct reparation to individual victims (although it may require repair work or construction work in the community, which may be regarded as a rough equivalent to the harm done). However, the essential point is that the work itself is not intended to be a punishment. The punitive element is that an order can be taken up between the above mentioned number of hours of an offender's spare time (at least one 7-hour day per week). The feasible element of rehabilitation has been claimed to come from either working alongside the public-spirited volunteers, or from working with the handicapped or other disadvantaged members of the community, although these were found as having little rehabilitative effect.[26] Both frequency in imposing community service by court and type of work undertaken, as well as work conditions, vary by circumscription.[27] Type of work undertaken, corroborated with laxity and inconsistency in enforcement practiced by some probation services (e.g., by allowing numerous failures to attend work appointments regularly, without returning the offender to court for breach proceedings), in other words, leaving to probation officers the authority and discretion which belong to courts, maintained community service order as a "soft" option. Therefore, the Government introduced in 1989 *The National Standards for Discipline and Breach Proceedings in Community Service*, which proclaimed the importance of "strict, predictable and consistent" breach policy and gave courts the power to adjudicate on the offender's excuses for non-attendance.[28] Accordingly, discretion of the probation service and its community service organizers, has been much reduced. Both media and politicians were responsible in promoting such a harsh line.[29] Apparently, these changes satisfied the government line of creating "tough and demanding" sanctions and answered the courts' complaints about heterogeneous practices and inconsistent enforcement.

Community service order was originally introduced as a main sentence but, according with *The CJA 1991*, it may be combined, when dealing with serious offenders, with other sentences or orders.

Breach of order may be punished by fine, revocation of order and punishment for original offense.

(e.5) **Combination order** is a new order in its own right, introduced by *The CJA 1991* (s. 11), and enforced in October 1992. It combines elements of both probation supervision (1 to 3 years) and community service (40 to 100 hours), and applies to any offender aged 16 or over. It is a separate entity from a sentence which combines two other orders. Although this is a novel element among the community sentences, it is worth mentioning that powers to mix probation and community service have been available in Scotland for some years.[30] Since it is a separate, single and integrated order of the court, its operation requires close liaison between probation and community service teams.

The aim in introducing the combination order was to provide a particularly demanding non-custodial sentence for some persistent offenders (especially property offenders) and to achieve their reintegration into the community through punishment (by means of positive and demanding unpaid work) and reparation to the community (by undertaking socially useful work).[31] Yet it is unclear why probation orders and community service orders might not cater to these offenders. *The National Standards 1992* did not provide clear characteristics for a certain group, but suggested only that amongst those offenders who might not be regarded as suitable for a combination order would be those whose lifestyle is particularly chaotic (e.g., as a result of drug or alcohol misuse) and who might therefore have particular difficulty in keeping to a community service work program; also, non-eligible would be those offenders with well-ordered lifestyles who have little need of, or little prospect of responding to, probation supervision. Combination orders that include demanding additional requirements within the probation element are particularly onerous and are likely to be difficult to complete, especially for younger offenders.[32] Thus, the outcome in practice will depend to a great extent on whether the courts do use the combination order for offenders who might previously have received custody and do not indulge certain offenders who would previously have received either probation or community service alone, and how they will deal with cases of breach.[33] A 1993 study on use of combination orders in court (made on 160 cases)[34] found that orders are usually imposed on offenders aged 21 or over (over 50% of orders), mostly related to property offenses (33% for burglary, 16% for theft or handling), traffic offenses (16%) and violent offenses (12%). In the same year, about 9,000 such orders were imposed.

The early termination may be considered only after completion of the community service element of the order, and then in accordance with the criteria for early termination of probation orders.

(e.6) **Curfew orders** require the offender aged 16 or over, convicted of any offense, to remain for up to 12 hours per day at a specified place, for a period of up to 6 months; *The CJA 1991*, s. 12. *Electronic monitoring* may be used should local arrangements have been approved (s. 13). The curfew arrangements must, so far as possible, not interfere with the times when the offender attends work or school, or conflict with the requirements of any other community order to which he may be subject. *Night restriction orders*, a form of curfew, have been available in juvenile courts since 1982, but they have little use (10 orders in 1987).[35] *The 1990 White Paper* argued that curfew orders would be a useful addition to the range of sentences in adult courts, reducing certain types of offenses (e.g., car thefts, pub brawls and other types of disorder) by keeping offenders away from particular places like shopping centers or pubs, or to keep them at home in the evenings or at weekends. Curfew orders by electronic monitoring were backed up by governmental logistic programs.[36] *The CJA 1991* allowed for curfew orders by electronic monitoring of the offender's whereabouts. The provisions have not yet been brought into effect but some experiment-trials in 1995 assessed the use of electronically monitored curfew orders as court sentences. Nonetheless, many probation officers opposed those initiatives motivating "costly ineffectiveness" and "degrading equal respect and dignity."[37] However, the power to enter into "contracts with other persons" for electronic monitoring of the offenders' whereabouts belongs exclusively to the Secretary of State; *The CJA 1991*, s. 13(3).

But courts have further alternatives to prevent offenders from frequenting specified places, under *The Licensed Premises (Exclusion of Certain Persons) Act 1980*, *The Public Order Act 1986* (exclusion orders relating to certain designated football matches) and *The Football Spectators Act 1989*.

A curfew order can be combined with a fine, a compensation order, an order for disqualification from driving or an order for forfeiture.

Post-judicial alternatives are forms of deinstitutionalization applied at post-sentencing stage, including *parole, work or educational release, halfway houses*, or *leaves on furlough, pardons* and *amnesty*. In addition, imprisonment itself, apart from its traditional full-time form, might require custody only at night (equivalent to *day-parole* or *work release*), or only during the day. Most of these measures can be applied in conjunction with or as a supplement to others.

These programs are not really alternatives to incarceration, but they can help to offset the damaging and dependency-producing effects of imprisonment, while reducing prison population on the other.

The most important of these post-judicial measures is **parole**, originally designed for long-term prisoners, and granted by the Parole Board. Under this scheme, prisoners are allowed to complete their sentence in the community, under parole supervision, provided that certain conditions and obligations carrying a wide range of restrictions on liberty are met.

With *The CJA 1991*, enforced on October 1, 1992, came a number of major changes in the parole system which were set successively, stemming from the recommendations of the Carlisle Review Committee,[38] and introducing the early release schemes, which provided for some support on release, in order to reduce the likelihood of reoffending.

All prisoners sentenced from October 1, 1992 to less than 4 years became automatically eligible for release after having served half of their sentence (except for any further days added for prison offenses). Two early release arrangements were designed for this category of offenders:

(a) *The Automatic Unconditional Release Scheme (AUR)*, according to which all inmates sentenced to under 12 months would be eligible, with no selection, and released automatically halfway through their sentence. There is no compulsory supervision, except for young offenders subject to statutory supervision;

(b) *The Automatic Conditional Release Scheme (ACR)*, according to which all inmates sentenced between 12 months and 4 years became eligible, with no selection, and released automatically halfway through their sentence on a license (issued on behalf of the Home Secretary by the Governor). They are subject to compulsory supervision up to three-quarters point of sentence. Some sex offenders may be supervised up to the 100% point of their sentence at the direction of the sentencing judge.

Inmates may be fined up to £1,000 by magistrates' courts for breaching the license conditions, recalled to prison for a maximum of 6 months (or the outstanding period of their license if that is less), or recalled by the Crown Court for the outstanding period of their license exceeding 6 months.

All inmates sentenced to 4 years and over became eligible for *The Discretionary Conditional Release Scheme (DCR)*, that is, for release on parole at the halfway point of sentence. All cases are considered by the Parole Board at regular intervals until the two-thirds point of sentence. Those not selected for parole within this period are automatically released on license at the two-thirds point. They are subject to supervision until the three-quarters point of sentence, whether they are released on parole or automatically at the two-thirds point (with the same exception for some sex offenders).

In addition, all prisoners will be "at risk" if they are convicted of an imprisonable offense committed during the last quarter of their sentence, of having all or part of the unexpired portion of their sentence added on to any new sentence that the court may impose.

Tracing "high-risk" cases and lowering the risk become important issues when there is a rise of uncertainty as to how this can be done in the context of prison life. The new parole system will ensure that cases identified by Parole Board panels as "high-risk" will receive supervision even if inmates are kept in prison until they have served two-thirds of their sentence, which could have a sizable impact for prison population in the future.[39]

Success depends on the feasibility with which those programs, designed to operate shortly before the end of the institutional treatment, prepare the offender for social reinsertion, and on quality of supervision.

3.2. UNITED STATES OF AMERICA

Among **pre-trial alternatives**, the most used are *bail* and *release on own recognizance*.

Bail is a monetary or other form of security given to insure the appearance of the defendant at every stage of the proceedings. It is aimed to relieve the defendant of imprisonment and the state of the burden of keeping him pending trial or hearing, and concomitantly to secure his appearance at the trial or hearing. However, by statute, certain defendants charged with particular offenses can be denied bail. The magistrate can reach the same result by setting a bail exceeding the defendant's financial capabilities.

Release on own recognizance usually requires the defendant's promise to appear before the authorities, though sometimes imposes special conditions (e.g., remaining in the custody of another, abiding by travel restrictions, etc.). In order to apply for release on own recognizance, the court must take into account the type of offense, the circumstances in which it was committed, the set of evidence, the offender's background and his criminal record, duration of residence in the community, and the record of appearance at court proceedings or of flight to avoid prosecution, or failure to appear at court proceedings.[40]

Fixing time-limits and other individual guarantees in the statutes does not automatically make justice administration more expeditious and equitable, though. If collateral measures, backed up by clear guidelines and adequate resources, will be properly planned and implemented, they will have the chance of an effective functioning.[41] Some of them might be: checking with the offender's financial means; requirement to reside at a specified address; restriction on leaving or entering a specified place or district without authorization; order to report periodically; surrender of passport or other ID's; an agency for supervision and assistance nominated by court.

Also worth considering would be the compensation schemes for defendants who spent time in custody pending trial and were subsequently acquitted.[42]

As to **sentencing alternatives**, only the recently developed forms will be summarized below, in order to avoid repetitions.

Restitution is usually ordered as a condition of a probationary sentence and sometimes as a sole sanction, with no additional penalties or requirements. In the United States, offenders are imposed either to pay back the victims (*monetary restitution*) or to serve the community as a compensation for their criminal acts (*community-service restitution*).[43] Financial restitution is ordered in about one third of all probation cases and averages US$ 3,400 per case; about 60% of all orders are paid in full within 3 years, while in 11% at least something is paid.[44] For community-service restitution there are allocated special centers of an open-prison type, where inmates must work to cover the damage their offense caused. Youths receiving restitution as a sole sanction are more likely to complete the order successfully and less likely to commit new offenses while under the jurisdiction of a restitution project.[45] Judges and probation officers have embraced the concept of restitution because it appears to benefit the victim of crime, the offender, the criminal justice system, and the society as well.[46] Financial restitution is inexpensive to administer, helps avoid stigma, and provides victim compensation. Community service work in schools, hospitals and nursing homes helps in saving thousands of dollars that otherwise would have been spent for offenders' maintenance in prisons, and concomitantly gives the feeling that equity has been returned to the justice system.

Most reviews rate restitution as a qualified success. A national survey of juvenile restitution programs revealed that in a single year some 17,000 orders were issued amounting to $2.6 million in monetary restitution, 340,000 hours of community service and 5,300 hours of direct service to victims work.[47] Estimates showed that almost 90% of the clients successfully completed their restitution orders and 86% had no subsequent contact with the justice system. Other research indicated that recidivism rates of those receiving restitution sentences were equal or lower than those receiving incarceration sentences.[48]

But the original enthusiasm for the restitution concept has been somewhat dampened by the concern that it has not lived up to its promise of being an alternative to incarceration. Critics charge that restitution merely serves to increase the proportion of persons whose behavior is regulated and controlled by the state. Restitution would add a burden to the people who would ordinarily have been given a relatively lenient probation sentence instead of a prison term.[49]

The practice of **mediation projects** has spread quickly and more than 20 states currently have similar projects.[50] The main objectives of mediation are: to recognize more effectively the victim's interest through damage reparation, to promote a genuine reconciliation between offenders and victims, and to make the offender explicitly aware of what he has done. There are a variety of mediation projects: *arbitration programs*, *citizen dispute settlement centers*, and *neighborhood justice centers*. Many of them are run by private organizations, not always backed by the judiciary. Generally, these private organizations find themselves on the margins of the criminal justice system, and the result is that mediation is only used with petty crime, except for the *victim-offender reconciliation programs*, where mediation takes place after conviction and the agreed compensation forms part of the sentence.[51] Allegedly, the closer the judiciary is involved with the projects, the greater the chance that mediation is presented as a real penal option.

The **fine** is a direct offshoot of the early common law practice of compensating the victim and the state for criminal acts. In the United States, fines are sanctions operating on a fixed-system base, according to the seriousness of the crime and the offender's criminal record. Most commonly, they are used in cases involving misdemeanors and lesser offenses, or in felony cases where the offender benefited financially.[52] A federal government study found that lower-court judges imposed fines alone or in tandem with other penalties in 86% of their cases, while superior-court judges imposed fines in 42% only.[53] However, fines are used sparingly, and they seem to be less popular than in Europe, mainly because judges are of the opinion that fining is too light a sentence for the wealthy and too heavy for the poor.[54] Most often, fines are imposed as an "add-on" to the "real" punishment, such as probation or incarceration, with the motivation that by using them as the sole punishment, at the levels necessary to achieve justice, they cannot be collected.

The **day-fine system** has been introduced on an experimental basis in various places, as an option for the short-term imprisonment. Successful collection for day-fines appears to depend on three factors: fines must not exceed the offender's paying capacity, installments must be limited as much as possible, and the payment period must not be too long.[55] Sometimes a collection agency is employed for collecting the payments, following the example of financial institutions, but more often, the probation service is involved in this task. The service may then reserve part of the money for investing in special probation projects for which financing is lacking.[56]

To the prototype of monetary punishments (i.e., fines, the court costs), some legislatures have recently added a range of **financial penalties**. The philosophy of this new trend is based on the popular belief that offenders should pay for the correctional services provided for by the state (e.g., the probation supervision fee), and some states have carried this to extremes.[57]

The expanding number of mandatory monetary sanctions often results in unrealistically high, and thus uncollectible, assessments imposed on an offender. Estimates showed that defendants fail to pay upwards of $2 billion in fines per year! Yet they could be used more often than they currently are if enforced more efficiently. In the early 1990s, experiments made in Bridgeport (Connecticut), Des Moines (Iowa) and Salem (Oregon) determined the effectiveness of the day-fine concept.[58] Judges often have inadequate information on the offender's ability to pay, resulting in defaults and contempt charges. They seemed to employ fines in a rational and fair manner: low-risk offenders are the ones most likely to receive fines instead of jail sentences, and the more serious the crime, the higher the amount of the fine. On the other hand, fixing the threshold of financial penalties according to the seriousness of the offense may impact negatively on success rate. The more serious the offense and the higher the fine, the greater the chances of failure to pay the fine and at being on risk of probation revocation. On the other hand, offenders who were fined are less likely to commit new crimes than those sentenced to imprisonment.[59]

Another alternative sanction with a financial basis is **forfeiture**. It involves the seizure of goods and instrumentalities related to the commission or outcome of a criminal act. For instance, federal law provides that after arresting drug traffickers, the government may seize the boats they used to import the narcotics, the cars used to carry the drugs overland, the warehouses in which the drugs were stored, and the homes paid for with the drug profits; upon conviction, the drug dealers lose permanent ownership of these "instrumentalities" of crime.[60] Initially applauded by officials as a hard-hitting way of seizing the illegal profits of drug law violators, forfeiture has been subsequently criticized because of government overzealousness in applying it.[61] Despite this drawback, forfeiture will likely continue to be used as an alternative sanction against such selective targets as drug dealers and white-collar criminals.

Another alternative, regarded by some theorists as "the most secure intermediate sanction"[62] is the sentence to a **residential community corrections** facility. These facilities are freestanding unsecured buildings that are not part of a prison and house pre-trial and adjudicated adults. The residents regularly depart to work, attend school, or participate in community corrections activities and programs. The community correctional facility is a vehicle to provide intermediate sanctions as well as a prerelease center for those about to be paroled from prison.[63] Probation departments and other correctional authorities have been charged with running the centers that serve as a pre-prison sentencing alternative. In addition, some centers are operated by private, nonprofit groups who receive referrals from the country or district courts. There are also residential pre-trial release centers for offenders who are in immediate need of social services before their trial and as halfway-back alternatives for both parole and probation violators who might otherwise have to be imprisoned. In this capacity, residential community corrections programs serve as a base from which offenders can be placed in outpatient psychiatric facilities, drug and alcohol treatment programs, job training, and so forth.

One recent development consists in employing the residential community corrections facilities as **day reporting centers**. Inspired by the English *daycenters*, day reporting centers have been conceived as a more effective reaction against property, drug related, traffic and violent offenses. Several facilities of is kind have been set up in Massachusetts, Connecticut, Minnesota and other states.[64] The centers have a spill-over function for prisons, by accommodating offenders in pre-trial detention and those waiting to be paroled. Therefore, they function as an option for early release, rather than as an alternative sanction. There are various ways of implementing projects of this sort (some centers demand 5 to 8 contacts per week, some others combine 3 contacts per week with electronic monitoring). Usually, the length of compulsory day attendance varies between 40 and 50 days. There are specific conditions imposed (e.g., compulsory treatment for drug addicts or alcoholics, curfew checks of offenders in the evening, following activity plans with educational value), and the level of supervision is higher than the one of the *intensive supervision programs*. Failure to comply with the requirements may result in the offender's return to prison. Day reporting centers have high rates of success with inmates released from secure confinement (70-80%) and medium success with probationers (50%). However, the former may be among the lowest risks in their groups, while the latter are generally program failures.

Despite the thousands of traditional and innovative residential community corrections programs in operation nationwide, there have been relatively few efforts made to evaluate their effectiveness. One reason is that programs differ considerably with respect to target population, treatment alternatives, and goals. While some are rehabilitation-oriented and operate under loose security, others are control-oriented and use such security measures as random drug and alcohol testing.

Probation is an institution with a long-lasting tradition in the United States.[65] It was originally promoted by John Augustus in Boston (Massachusetts) in 1841, as a scheme for preventing reoffending, applicable to petty offenders (usually, alcoholics and thieves), and subsequently expanded nationwide. In time, major changes were set in train, some of them[66] deserving particular attention: *shock probation* (a combination of probation with short-term custody); *probation with restitution* (both financial or symbolic); *probation with residence* in treatment centers or hostels; *probation with employment opportunities*; and *probation with outreach programs* which maintains continuous contacts with the offender's environment.[67]

The extensive use of paraprofessionals and volunteers from the community, and full involvement of local and district rehabilitation councils or other citizens' groups act as bridges between the criminal justice system, the social service agencies and the population as a whole, and constitute significant new developments in the area. In fact, the ultimate goal, the offender's reintegration into the community, means an effective use of public services combined with the community's full involvement in this process, at both central, local and state levels of the executive.

Another issue relates to the very concept and practice of "supervision." It is not always possible to find the proper balance between the competing elements of control and social work. In those cases, supervision becomes more informal, performed by persons with no particular skills and professional experience, or by local authorities other than the courts or probation officers themselves, and so ensuring a broader community participation in implementing such a measure. Whatever the emphasis, probation goals should be clearly defined so as to identify the service needs on a systematic and sustained basis.[68]

Community service was initiated in 1966 as a penalty for traffic offenses. At present, it is largely used for white-collar offenders, juvenile delinquents and petty offenders. In practice, the risk for breaching the sentence grows in direct proportion with the number of hours imposed.[69] As a result, community service is, unlike in Europe, scarcely used as a sentence in its own right, but as a supplement to other sentences instead, or, if used for more serious crimes, as part of the alternative package.

Among **post-judicial alternatives**, the most controversial institution is **parole**, linked to indeterminate sentences as an expression of the rehabilitative ideal (e.g., the prisoner is granted parole when he is "ready" to be released). The core of parole (indeterminate sentence),[70] its very process (i.e., eligibility criteria, selection and revocation), the great amount of discretion and arbitrariness involved in decisions, as well as the disparity and the inconsistency in its application, have all been subject to severe criticism.[71] Some critics called for appropriate guidelines in order to structure, delimit and regulate discretion,[72] while others suggested a more radical reform, namely an abandonment of indeterminate sentence and parole.[73] As a result, 7 states abolished both parole and indeterminate sentences, and 15 other states adopted new sentencing guidelines.[74]

Typical conditions for parole include periodic meetings with parole officers, foregoing the possession of weapons, and not associating with known criminals.

3.3. THE BRITISH COMMONWEALTH

3.3.1. CANADA. **Mediation projects**, also known as *victim-offender reconciliation programs*, are imposed on both adults and juveniles. Usually, offenders with previous convictions are eligible. In Quebec, mediation is limited to the first offenders only.

Compensation (with unpaid work) is a requirement included in 75% of conditional sentences.[75]

Community service is not used as a substitute for imprisonment. The sanction is mostly imposed as a special condition of a conditional sentence, usually for minor and non-violent offenses (unlike England), and its enforcement depends on the specific regulations of each province. The average length varies from 49 to 60 hours, and in some provinces the hours can be converted into fines (on a rate of Can.$ 5 per working hour). In the past two decades, several trial projects with low-risk detainees-to-be were started in Ontario, which have impacted significantly upon the recidivism rate (lowered to 18-23% in the year following the completion of community service orders).[76]

3.3.2. AUSTRALIA. **Probation**, as outlined by the 1884 Berenger draft law in France, was adopted in Queensland, in 1886. Later on, Queensland replaced suspension of the execution of sentence with suspension of the imposition of sentence, a practice which had spread itself throughout the whole colony.

Community service orders, under various names and modalities, are also carried out in every state.[77]

3.3.3. NEW ZEALAND. **Probation** was introduced in 1886, following the 1878 Massachusetts model in America, with the difference that the measure was applicable to minor offenses and for first offenders only.

Both **periodic detention** and **weekend detention** consist in a limited deprivation of liberty, with some contact with the outside world. In practice, these measures do not remove the offender from the community but allow him to continue to work outside and to maintain his family ties. Periodic detention entails a sentence to perform supervised restitutive work within the community, in conjunction with a limited deprivation of liberty on weekends or weekday nights. It is similar in may ways to the restitution schemes and the community service orders.[78]

3.3.4. OTHER COUNTRIES. In Jamaica, **probation** was introduced under the Anglo-Saxon influence. The country is engaged in a serious effort to make the probationary system work properly. This is due, to a great extent, to the domestic high crime rate and the prison overcrowding. Probation work is coordinated by a Department of Correctional Service whose staff counts more than a hundred of probation officials. On the whole, probation order has a low rate of applicability (3% of the total sentences).

The Criminal Justice (Reform) Act of 1977 introduced a new system of **suspended sentence**.[79]

Constant efforts have been made to increase efficiency of **community service** in dealing with offenders.[80]

CHAPTER 4

OTHER LEGAL SYSTEMS

4.1. THE ARAB COUNTRIES

In Egypt and Sudan, statistical data indicate that over 60% of custodial sentences passed for less serious offenses,[1] a reason for which non-custodial alternatives should be given more credit.

Restitution plays an important role as a primary function of punishment, being backed by Islamic traditions, e.g. *enforced restitution* to the victim.

Fine and *probation* are two alternative sanctions frequently used by courts.

Fine is employed in combination with restitution, and takes the form of a property forfeiture, rather than a monetary sanction. Complicated restitution scales, stemming from old customs and traditions, operate in relation with fines in assets (especially animals).

Probation has encountered criticism from theorists and lawmakers, because it has allegedly failed to avoid recidivism.

The process of implementing non-custodial alternatives, especially of Western origin, is generally stalled by domestic legal customs, but specific programs for authorities within criminal justice administration, focusing on the trumps of such alternatives like cost-reducing or the speedy social reintegration could eventually facilitate this goal.

4.2. ASIA

In many Asian countries, alleviating prison overcrowding is a top priority. The number of defendants waiting in pre-trial custody ranges between 30-50% of inmates (30% in South Korea and Thailand, 40% in India, over 50% in Pakistan and Sri Lanka). Accordingly, non-custodial sanctions, such as *suspended prosecution, release on bail, fine, suspended sentence, probation, parole* and *pardon* are welcomed by lawmakers, who seek various solutions to improve and expand them.

Traditionally, **pre-trial diversion** schemes provide for extrajudiciary settlements in petty crime cases, deemed as less complicated by common people. In Iran, the local disputes are settled by the *houses of equity* in the rural areas and the *arbitration councils* in the cities. In the Philippines, the local authorities (*barangay*) are responsible for maintaining law and order, and for settling minor disputes, cutting short considerably the backlog of cases in courts. Similar functions activate through the *conciliation boards* in Sri Lanka and the *village panchayat* in India.

In countries with discretionary prosecution (Japan, South Korea), district attorneys are authorized to **suspend prosecution** at their own discretion, if "the interest of society" so imposes, even though there is sufficient evidence to prove the guilt. In Indonesia, the Attorney General may initiate the procedure of prosecution for political reasons if "public order" is deemed to be better served this way. In the rural areas, police officers may divert petty offenders from criminal trial if there is a damage compensation. Settling issues by compromise is a solution favored by local customary law (*adat*). In Myanmar (Burma), compromise between parties prevents prosecution.

Even though suspension of prosecution proves effective for minor offenses, its arbitrariness needs to be explicitly guidelined and supervised, in order to avoid abuse and corruption in justice administration.

As to **bail**, some national statutes divide offenses in bailable and non-bailable (Bangladesh, India, Malaysia, Myanmar, Pakistan, and Singapore). Thus, bail is granted with or without sureties for bailable offenses, while it may be granted at the judge's own discretion for non-bailable offenses. Yet high rates of pre-trial custody in many Asian countries prove that bail is not given full credit.

Among the **sentencing alternatives**, the most utilized are *fines*, *suspended sentences*, and *probation orders*, accompanied by a system of traditional non-custodial sanctions.

Fine is imposed upon a great number of offenders in the most developed countries (96%, in Japan, 92%, in Singapore, 65%, in South Korea), while in the less developed ones, since many offenders are indigent and cannot afford to pay, courts do not take it as the top alternative for imprisonment. Instead, the short-term custody rate is reduced by using community-based corrections for insolvent offenders. Sri Lanka, for instance, introduced *compulsory work centers* and *day-fines* for indigent offenders.

Suspended sentence is most often a substitute for short-term imprisonment. It is statutory provided, with elements of supervision, in Japan, South Korea, Indonesia, and Thailand, and sometimes covers more than half of the custodial sentences (62% in Japan, 51% in South Korea). In Afghanistan, Iraq, Nepal, and South Korea, suspendees are given support and guidance from after-care services and charitable organizations. South Korea and Thailand have provided schemes of a similar nature as the European suspended sentence system or the *suspension of imposition of sentence*. In the 1970s, Sri Lanka restricted temporarily the court prerogative to suspend the execution of imprisonment, due to the high crime rate and the political unrest in the country at the time.

Absolute discharge, **conditional discharge,** which act as a suspension of imposition or execution of sentence, and **bind-overs** are also frequently applied as imprisonment substitutes in India, Pakistan, and Singapore.

Probation is regarded as one of the most important and promising alternatives to imprisonment. In Bangladesh, China (Hong Kong), Malaysia, and Singapore, probation is ordered by the court as an independent sentencing alternative. The court can revoke the order in case of breach of the conditions imposed and pass instead a sentence for the first offense. In India, a probation system was introduced in the early 1920s, but it developed slowly due to a complex combination of geographical, cultural and financial factors.

In some countries, such as China (Hong Kong) and Singapore, probation is used extensively, for any offender except those who commit serious crimes (treason, murder), but satisfactory termination is recorded for only 55% adults and 72% juveniles. In Japan, the probation officer may discharge from supervision the probationers who adjust satisfactorily their behavior in the community. This practice appears to have some impact among offenders, since about 70% are discharged yearly from supervision for good community adjustment, and only some 6% have their probation revoked for misbehavior.

There are also some dysfunctions precluding the satisfactory use of probation. In Malaysia, lack of guidelines outlining specific duties for probation officers and the overlapping prerogatives leave little room for an effective supervision. Besides, many police officers strongly disfavor probation system, regarding too "soft" an option. As a result, courts appear to prefer bind-overs or other sanctions to probation. In Bangladesh, there are no effective programs for treating offenders in society. The number of probation officers is limited to several dozens (some 20 probation officers throughout the country have to supervise over 500 probationers), the budget is limited, and, moreover, public opinion is not stimulated to cooperate. In Thailand there is a similar situation: a quasi-total absence of human resources (only about 30 full-time probation officers were appointed by the Ministry of Justice), turns probation into a *rara avis* of the alternatives.

On the other hand, countries where probation is extensively and successfully implemented have developed a strong voluntary sector. In Japan, the national probation service, counting as much as 1,000 professional officers, is backed up by over 45,000 volunteer probation workers. The limited caseload (2 cases per officer), enables them to stay in constant and close contact with their clients. In addition, there are also over 500 fraternal associations with over 8,000 members and over 1,000 women's associations for rehabilitation aid counting more than 200,000 members, backed up by volunteer probation workers and sometimes probationers and parolees, who offer assistance and counseling. In China (Hong Kong), the volunteer scheme for probation formally commenced in 1976; its primary goal was to promote a more positive public attitude towards reforming the offenders, and to increase community involvement in crime prevention and post-judicial treatment. The public response was encouraging, since over 15 pairs of probationers and volunteers (including teachers, nurses, students, social workers) have been matched since then, and their number is expanding. Extensive volunteering is also successfully practiced in Singapore and the Philippines, while in India and Sri Lanka volunteers are employed on an experimental basis. For many countries with a shortage of probation officers and social workers, volunteering and compartmentalizing volunteers' activity might be the solution for the future.

Other alternatives to imprisonment include: **exile**, in Iran (to places designated by court, and enforced under police supervision) and the Philippines (access prohibited in the surrounding area, usually 15 miles, of the designated place); housing in **protective hostels**, for prostitutes, in Japan and India; **home confinement** for 3-month convicts, in Thailand; **flagellation** (whipping), in Bangladesh, China (Hong Kong), Pakistan, Singapore and Sri Lanka (seldom used), **publishing the sentence**, in Indonesia.

Special alternatives are available for certain types of offenders, such as: *juveniles*, to **referral to reform and training schools**, in China (Hong Kong), Japan, the Philippines, and South Korea, to **borstal (reformatory) schools**, in Bangladesh, India and Myanmar, or to **remand homes (probation hostels)**, in Malaysia and Sri Lanka; *the mentally disordered*, to **confinement in medical institutions**, in Japan; *drug addicts*, to **centers for narcotics addicts**, in China (Hong Kong) (6 to 18-month treatment, plus 12-month after-care), **hospitalization**, in Japan (1 to 6 months), commitment to public and private **drug rehabilitation centers**, in Malaysia, the Philippines, Singapore and Thailand. Specialized volunteer agencies assist and counsel in the rehabilitation process, like "The Society for the Aid and Rehabilitation of Drug Addicts" in China (Hong Kong) or "The Anti-Narcotic Association" in Singapore.

The **extramural treatment during imprisonment** deserves a special mention. Open or semi-open prisons, characterized by the absence of walls and other physical measures of precaution against escape, have been developed in many Asian countries. Usually organized as *outside work camps* or *farms*, they are suited to meet the needs of the respective region, ecologically, economically and in terms of sound social policy. In India, long-term prisoners are sent to open prisons after they have served part of their sentence in jail. In Japan, traffic offenders were originally targeted for open prisons but currently other groups are targeted, as well. In the Philippines, *penal colonies* are established on a permanent basis; in addition, there are several *penal farms* attached to prisons. Relieving prison overcrowding and exploiting the vast natural resources of this multi-island state appear to have been the main forces leading to the creation of the *penal colonies*.[3] In Sri Lanka there are *open prison camps* for short-term convicts and for the long-term ones who have served one half of their sentence, which function as *pre-release centers*. Inmates are employed mostly in agricultural work and animal husbandry. Participation in community development projects is also encouraged. Similar experiments, with the same encouraging effects on rehabilitation, have been initiated in Thailand.

Broadly, the open prison programs are considered to be successful. In India (Uttar Pradesh), follow-up surveys reported rates of over 75% of ex-inmates settling down satisfactorily, while other countries recorded lower reconviction rates.

Work release programs, allowing daytime work outside the prison for selected inmates, are employed in Japan (implemented in open or semi-open prisons and juvenile training schools) and South Korea (for inmates with vocational training in mechanical engineering). Rigorous selection helps keep the escape rate low, and for many inmates these programs bring additional income for their families and extra ways to compensate the victims.

Furlough, aiming at strengthening the inmate's family ties and increasing adaptability in an open milieu, is practiced in Iraq (a 5-day home leave every 3 months, after serving one third of the sentence but not less than 1 year), India (for good behavior), South Korea (up to 3 weeks, granted for important family events or serious emergencies), and Sri Lanka (7 days every 6 months in the last 12 months of imprisonment, to cope with daily life problems).

In the Asian tradition, local communities and organizations are particularly important for crime prevention and treatment of offenders (e.g., conciliation councils for petty criminal claims, volunteering in probationary supervision). They compensate, more or less efficiently, for the unfavorable effects generated by the lack of human and economic resources, creating conditions for a better expansion of those programs in the area.

4.3. AFRICA

After World War II, colonial administrations, particularly the British one, used **probation** as a means to reform the juvenile delinquents serving in adult prisons, but this practice had little success. In the Congo, the shortage of specialized staff kept the "supervised freedom for juveniles" far from the type of close supervision type that probation would normally imply.[4]

Ghana, Kenya, Nigeria and Uganda have established **reformatory schools** for juveniles under 18 years old patterned after the English *borstals*, **approved schools** for teens aged 10 to 16, and **remand homes** for juveniles in pre-trial stages.

In the early 1900s, Kenya, Nigeria and Tanzania organized **prison farms** handling specific activities for inmates, like farm training, tailoring, carpentry and bricklaying.[5]

After the independence years, in the 1960s, the African states had to mold their customary law and the existing colonial Western legal structures into feasible models for the modern way of life. A suggested prototype was the **community-based center**, designed for short-term imprisonment, where the community would complement the custodial functions and the local companies would serve as experimental bases for behavioral change. The skilled people in the community (local chiefs, farmers, traders, fishermen, merchants, craftsmen) would act as counselors and managers for the community-based center. The type of activities, both residential and non-residential, would be diverse and in accordance with the local conditions and the clients' needs.[6]

How far viable elements of customary law can be taken over by the modern penal systems remains a question with no clear answer at the moment. However, countries like Somalia and Tanzania are making considerable efforts to harmonize their colonial penal legacies with the local legal customs, in order to create a new and more dynamic national law.

CONCLUSIONS

The autonomous development of non-custodial alternatives emerged from a process of progressive humanization in the criminal justice system. In most countries, efforts to limit the use of custody were made by amending criminal statutes and introducing sentencing guidelines. The frequent use of non-custodial sanctions will ease offender rehabilitation but the community will have to increase its responsibility and involvement accordingly. On the other hand, promoting alternative sanctions in all three stages of the judicial process (pre-trial, sentencing and post-judicial) as part of the sentencing reform policy, should be seen as an attempt to surmount some socio-economic and financial difficulties generated by long-term custodial sentences, the increase of prison population, and the high costs of incarceration.

The goals of alternative sanctions were initially offender-oriented, focusing on the resocializing character of the punishment; the offender could compensate the victim and society by making restitution to the community or working in its benefit. Mediation, restitution and compensation, and community service bear a sense of reparation to the breached legal rule redress and of vindication for the victim. But the stronger emphasis on victim's rights, in a growing influence on the sentencing process, contributed to the gradual shift away from rehabilitation toward restitution and public protection, regarded as the genuine goals of punishment. Sanctions like intensive probation supervision, electronic monitoring, house arrest, and residential community centers have a definite element of control and their primary function is to guarantee compliance with the imposed conditions. In spite of the frequent use of alternatives, judges are sometimes inclined to turn them into substitutes for other non-custodial sanctions, widening the net of the criminal justice system. Another pitfall consists in the growing number of special conditions, which increase, in fact, the risk of breaching them, with the perspective for the offender to be sent back to prison. As a result, many convicts prefer to passively serve in custody instead of being imposed substitutes with hard privacy intruding requirements. In spite of the overall presence of the retributive elements in the non-custodial sanctions, the rehabilitative character is bolder at some alternatives, which gives a somewhat contradictory image on the whole.

Some general trends are noticeable when surveying the penal policies from various geographic areas. Totalitarian societies tend to promote severe sanctioning systems, based on long-term custody and highly retributive substitutes. Many developing countries, where community plays an important role, prefer to apply community-based sanctions. In the developed countries, with a wide range of non-custodial substitutes, alternatives do not function all the time as substitutes to imprisonment but rather as alternatives to each other. This substantiates the old desideratum of reconciling the two polar tendencies, namely to monitor the increase of the prison population and the associated costs and, at the same time, to satisfy the public demands for more adequate punishments.

These experiences teach us several lessons. The range of alternatives is wide but contradictory at the same time. For the lawmaker seeking new models, not only custodial sentences but also alternative sanctions are to be ranked, whereby not only different sorts of sanctions but also the relative harshness of the sanction must be taken into account (e.g., the level of fine, the length of community service, the intensity of probation supervision, and so forth). The lawmaker should know from the very beginning what type of criminal policy he is going to adopt, and which category of offenders will be targeted by the alternatives that are to be implemented. If emphasis is to be put on rehabilitation, then the offender's needs and requirements should be regarded as paramount; if focus is on reparation, the victim becomes the main actor, and if the stress is on retribution, then the *just desert* goal of punishment plays the leading role. In order to substantiate one or more of these objectives, it is equally important that the judiciary should use the alternative sanctions in a balanced manner and in accordance with the general trends of the moment in the society. Such a balanced option, that best illustrates the everlasting tensions between the rehabilitative ideals, the victim reparation, and the *just desert* principles is probation.

PART TWO

PROBATION ORDER

CHAPTER 5

PROBATION AND SUSPENDED SENTENCE: PROS AND CONS

From a comparative point of view, probation is a combination of two elements: a conditional suspension of punishment, and personal care and supervision, two factors which the original suspended sentence, developed mostly in the civil law countries, ignored completely. While this is specific for countries with a classical probation system, like the United Kingdom and the United States, in continental Europe the two elements have had an existence of their own. As a reaction to the promising start the Anglo-American probation had in the mid-nineteenth century, suspended sentence or the *sursis*, as a suspension of its execution pure and simple, was firstly adopted by the Belgian and the French statutes in 1888 and 1891 respectively, then taken over by the rest of Europe and subsequently spread to Latin America. Organized personal care and supervision of offenders, with, but more often without, the power of the law behind it, in the forms of a protective supervision or the *liberte surveille*, was regarded as a prerequisite of the modern court law, related mostly to juveniles. The system worked out that way for the whole first half of the twentieth century. Such an evolution, that disfavored a combination of the two elements of probation, was therefore improper for a device like adult probation. Theorists and lawmakers in continental Europe saw probation less in terms of the English tradition, as rooted in the ancient contract of recognizance (a creation of caselaw), or in terms of the American philanthropic efforts done in the nineteenth century, than in terms of the current written legal norms, in accordance with the civil law tradition of the European countries. In Massachusetts, "the cradle of probation," John Augustus began his bold experiments in human rescue work with adult drunkards. In England, the pioneers of the unofficial probation, Matthew Davenport Hill and E. W. Cox were interested in a new device for dealing with juvenile delinquents;[1] when *The Probation of First Offenders Act 1887* in England led to a demand for social workers who were to undertake the supervising function, the police court missionaries, with their experience in preventive and remedial work with adults, filled the gap. Both in England and the United States, probation was not only a typical educative measure for juvenile delinquents but a remedial method for adult offenders, too.

In the early 1900s and especially after the World War I, suspended sentence was periodically added to, and incorporated many elements from, the probation system. After World War II, the Anglo-American probation impacted significantly the penal policies and the statutory law in the civil law countries. In 1944, courts in Sweden were invested to suspend either the imposition or the execution of the sentence. Belgium and France, the countries of the classical *sursis*, focused on training social workers for criminal justice administration and encouraged practical experiments of institutionalized supervision in post-trial and post-execution stages (Belgium in 1946, France in 1950).[2] In the early 1950s, Germany experimentally attached social workers for social inquiries and supervision to the juvenile courts, and in 1953 its Penal Code was amended in order to facilitate the development of a national probation service.[3]

In 1958, France introduced suspension with supervision or conditional sentence (the *sursis avec mise a l'epreuve*), an institution much closer related to the classical probation. The device imposed certain requirements to the offender and placed him under assistance and control. In 1975, Italy adopted a similar system. Yet conditional sentence, even imposing certain requirements and having a regime of supervision, has always embodied the spirit of the original ordinary suspended sentence, seen as a measure of individualizing the penalty rather than a method of treatment. Besides, in the continental criminal procedure pre-trial investigations are carried on by prosecutors (or the *juges d'instruction*, in the French system), while in the common law system social inquiries are made in the interval between sentence and conviction, so that reports may be read to magistrates only after the defendant has been found guilty and thus after the tension of the trial stage has receded. This is because social inquiries and pre-sentence reports are indispensable tools for the treatment of offenders. Then, the two alternatives differ in the timing of the suspension of punishment and the type of voluntary cooperation done by non-professional social workers.

An overview of the past hundred of years reveals a process of alternate trends of polarity and merger between probation and suspended sentence. The first stage, in the last quarter of the nineteenth century, was marked by polarity. Suspended sentence entailed suspension of imposition of the sentence, while probation entailed suspension of both execution and imposition of the sentence, and was accompanied by a system of supervision or assistance. In a second stage, between wars, there was an increasing closeness between probation and suspended sentence, with a growing influence of the former on the latter. After 1945, the two systems became amalgamated, with probation still prevailing, mostly in the Scandinavian countries. The disappearance of the classical suspended sentence (the *sursis simple*) was predicted by some, at the time when some U.S. state courts had just been abilitated to suspend either the imposition or the execution of the sentence. In the 1960s and the 1970s, with the emergence of the radical criminology and the therapeutic models in criminal justice, the two devices again distanced themselves from each other. Suspended sentence regained its initial function as a means of individualizing the penalty and as a "judicial favor" while probation kept its feature as being a method of treatment and rehabilitation. In England, implementation of suspended sentence was not particularly successful; the courts used it excessively and combined it with other alternatives having different targets, which eventually stimulated the reoffending rate. In the 1980s and the 1990s, the crime rate increased and the merging process came out again. Probation intensified its retributive role (in the United Kingdom it became a penalty in its own right in 1991), while adde to suspended sentence were new statutory elements involving assistance and surveillance (especially in Eastern Europe, whose precarious prison facilities, inherited from the former Communist authorities, favored new rehabilitationist trends). Currently, the process presents similar modulations, since the last hour tendencies reveal a new comeback for probation, from the retributive model to the values of the traditional social work and therapy.[4]

In terms of effectiveness, a comparison between probation and suspended sentence is difficult to make, since the granting conditions for each vary. Besides, apart from the situation in the common law countries, where suspended sentence lacks popularity, in the civil law countries there is a competition even between the different versions of suspended sentence, namely the no-supervision standard type and conditional sentence. In Western Europe, for instance, the standard suspended sentence, as a traditional alternative, took the leads in the beginning, then fell off due to the extensive use of conditional sentence. Some hastened to predict the end of the classical suspended sentence, but no such thing has happened so far. On the contrary, statistics reveal that the numerous breaches of conditions imposed by conditional sentence restimulated the use of no-supervision suspended sentence.[5] In Eastern Europe, conditional sentence has been adopted relatively late and the courts do not use it very often,[6] though the situation may very well change in the near future.

Interestingly enough is the continental lawmaker's philosophy when dealing with the legislative preeminence of one or the other of the two alternatives in discussion. On one hand, the Anglo-American model has been recognized as a strong stimulus for rehabilitation and having the great advantage of sparing the offender of a disreputable sentence and its consequences. On the other hand, one might interpret its lenience as an abdication from the *just desert* principle, a kind of "blank check" given to the offender. Besides, conditional suspension of punishment would result in losing or destroying the evidence in time. Moreover, the efficiency of the penalty individualization, which in the civil law relies to a great extent on the oral debates, would definitely be affected if sentence were passed by a different panel. The current Franco-Belgian system would eliminate these flaws. Thus, in case of a suspended execution of the sentence, the fact that the offender is already convicted would generate a stronger and more productive psychological effect on his future behavior. Likewise, the proceedings would be much simpler, since, in case of reoffending, there is no need for a new fact finding in court, so the risk of losing evidence is minimized. Finally, such an option would satisfy to a higher extent the public opinion's feelings for justice.[7]

Irrespective of the number of pros and cons, the crucial point stands, as mentioned already, in the distinct philosophies guiding the criminal policy of each country, or, more specifically, in the legal nature and aims attributed to each of the alternatives in question: means of deterrence and individualization of penalty ("judicial favor") or treatment for rehabilitation ("social therapy").

The civil law countries have always looked for improving the regime of conditional sentence without abdicating from the general principles emerging from their legal tradition, in fact reflecting in the last instance a certain mass psychology. Innovators in the Continent struggled many times against the old traditionalists who regarded the foreign institutions as being juridically heretical.[8] Yet most of the comparative studies showed that the Anglo-American pattern of suspension of the imposition of sentence and of supervision has constantly influenced the continental statutory law. Apparently, the caselaw follows a similar direction. However, the continental legal traditions, still strong, will certainly influence the various theoretical approaches in this area.

CHAPTER 6

LEGAL NATURE AND FUNCTIONS

According to the classical philosophy of probation, the average offender is not actually a dangerous criminal or a menace to society. Probation supporters suggested that prison would become the new reference point for the convict who was refused a community correction. The convict would be forced to interact with hardened criminals and the "ex-con" label would prohibit him from a successful adjustment to society. On the contrary, probation would be a "second chance" by offering close supervision carried out by trained personnel, which would sensibly facilitate the offender's adjustment to community standards.

Initially, probation was devised as a means of saving people from the degradation of a prison sentence, a *let off*.[1] Assumably, the offender, realizing that society gave him the chance to make amends by avoiding the punishment he had merited, would be moved by gratitude and penitence.

Field research proved that this assumption was in some respects over-confident. In fact, very few offenders believe that they merit the humiliation and exposure of an arrest, a charge or the public blame. Probation was to be seen as a new *preventive sentencing option*, a *sui generis* method of dealing with offenders or a "third way," distinct from a discharge or custody.[2]

Later on, certain theorists and some practitioners believed that probation would replace the functions of a punishment, and leniency was disregarded. Arguably, the offender needed a wholesome reminder that he could not offend with impunity. In the United Kingdom, *The Criminal Justice Act 1967* empowered courts to order disqualification from driving and endorsed the license in addition to probation. Both these measures are means of restitution and prevention, encouraging the offender to accept his responsibilities to others. They also have a punitive element, making probation more publicly acceptable where the offender needs treatment in the open but they consequently inflict serious harm by restraint. The offender now perceives the probation order as a punishment *per se*: he is required to keep in touch with his supervisor, receive visits, attend various recuperative programs. In short, he has the feeling of a continuous burden pressing over him throughout the duration of the order.[3] Even though such requirements and restrictions are aimed to help rather than punish, they make probation far more exacting than, for instance, a fine, which can be paid and forgotten. Far from being a let off, the offender is constantly reminded, if only by implication, of his offense and its consequences. This goal is particularly stressed by some courts and probation officers who deliberately make probation as unpleasant as possible, e.g., by asking to report at inconvenient hours, requesting to travel long distances to make appointments with the probation officer and to pay the fares, and maintaining military discipline at the office. But such methods have allegedly little remedial effect for the offender's personality. On the contrary, they make the probationer think that life is hard, he is unlucky, and the next time he should not get caught again. Criminological literature has abundantly emphasized the limits of the punitive policies as a method of crime reduction.

Another interpretation, apparently attuned with the original spirit of the institution, is probation as *treatment*, where psychology and psychiatry offer scientific or curative approaches alongside the purely legal or the ethical ones. From this angle, delinquency becomes highly individualized. Accordingly, an effective treatment has to be individually planned in order to meet individual needs. A positive function of probation is the probation officer's ability to arouse and redirect the offender's emotions.[4] Also, a good treatment develops factors conducive to moral health. But concentration upon the relationship between offender and officer as the core of treatment could have some pitfalls. It may become unduly exclusive, it may take insufficient account of the natural relationships in the offender's life, with much stronger and longer effects upon him, for good and ill. It may lead to undue dependence upon a particular officer, resulting in breakdown when his support is withdrawn. Also, there is a potential risk of becoming too familiar with staff, which could at some stage endanger the probationer's liberty through misunderstanding.[5]

While some offenders need, in addition to the single relationship with the officer, the support and stimulation of group treatment, others need protection and continuous contacts in a hostel. All these possibilities do not deny but supplement the value of a direct relationship with the probation officer, enlarging the scope of the treatment.

After the 1980s, probation service in England has become, with government support, an agency of more punishment. Without breaking with its traditional role as an agent of social control, as some asserted, it is clearly no longer a purely welfare service. If in the early twentieth century probation used to be imposed "instead of a sentence," the current legislation has given to probation service the power to punish people by restraining their freedom. The tendency to accommodate the traditional social work rehabilitative values with the government correctionalist philosophy was frequently put under question.[6] *The Criminal Justice Act 1982* imposed curfew conditions and community service orders for both juveniles and adults, and amended the status of bail and probation hostels. The rationale was that a large set of community corrections will substantially reduce the population in custody centers (prisons, bail hostels, remand homes). The Green and White Papers[7] urged that community punishments should become more disciplinary, correctional and restrictive. The idea of a "punishment in the community," also backed by mass media,[8] has been strongly criticized for coming up against the rehabilitative ideal, very dear to the probation staff.[9] The official doctrine eventually compromised by offering a dual notion of punishment, based on both the classical retributivism (focused on the gravity of the offense) and the neo-positivist consequentialism (focused on the consequences of preventing new crimes).[10] *The Criminal Justice Act 1991* settled in a definite way the issue of whether probation should be a punishment, another form of treatment, a reparative measure or a preventive sentencing option. Probation has been converted into a sentence in its own right, being implicitly considered as another form of punishment. In practice, one still makes the distinction between the formally stated obligations and the daily enforcement by the front line staff, who are directly involved in supervision but reluctant to punish clients unnecessarily. Expectedly, discretionary practices will continue to be constructed for personal and professional reasons, despite the attempts at centralizing and standardizing the punitive enforcement decisions.

In the United States, professional commitment to the rehabilitative ideal
was virtually unchallenged from the late nineteenth century until the 1960s. In
the 1970s and the 1980s, the "welfare approach" was, in various terms,
severely criticized as ineffective.[11] Initially, there was a normative or
neoclassical front which questioned the assumptions of rehabilitation as a
prominent goal for criminal sentencing. Neoclassicism advocated the so-
called *justice model*, that is the return from a sentencing based on the
perceived offender characteristics to a sentencing based on the offense,
determinate sentences, and the voluntary participation in rehabilitation
programs.[12] Punishment, in a neoclassicist sense (equity, proportionality and
fairness) do not identify itself with pure vengeance; in practice, it may support
ameliorative services but it prohibits coercion against offenders. Unlike the
neoclassicists, who were reaffirming the normative order in society by
promoting punishment based on desert, other analysts called for sentences
emphasizing the offender's restraint for purposes of deterrence (specific or
general) and incapacitation (isolation or surveillance).[13] Incapacitationists'
policy goals got wide public support and dominated for a while the political
agenda.[14] Then, the empirical research, well-publicized, backed with data the
idea of a low impact of probation on future criminal behavior, and of an
effective intervention on its own, which would suffice, except for some top
priority problems for offenders, such as housing, finances, jobs or illness.[15]
The *empirical attitude* became a reference point for the widespread claims
that "nothing works." In spite of some later studies which found correctional
programs as being effective when adequately implemented and appropriately
directed toward responsive client groups,[16] professional and popular support
for the rehabilitative ideal declined appreciably and appears not to have
recovered much ever since.[17] Finally, some critics invoked existing
fundamental economic contradictions and the unavailability of proper
material resources[18] or increased class conflict.[19]

Predictions about probation have been and will be made but the major
tendency remains the conflict between custody (enforcement) and treatment
(rehabilitation), frequently cited by literature.[20] Nowadays, the conflict runs
towards a certain fusion between the *justice model* and the *welfare model*,
with compromises from both sides. The community of supervision officers,
who had previously supported reintegration and rehabilitation as the goal of
probation and other community corrections, has shifted its attitude in the

direction of enforcement and protection.[21] The change is significant in view of public feeling which constantly favored enforcement and surveillance as goals for the adult probation system. If the criminal sanction remains in the background for most of the probation officer's work, the use of this tool is subtly altered, as concepts of treatment become more sophisticated. Assumably, a dual goal system will prevail, permitting elements of both enforcement and rehabilitation to coexist within the same system.

The extent to which probation officers support a dual goal of enforcement and rehabilitation during a time in which public attitudes appear to favor community protection has been spotlighted by some research.[22]

The polar relation between the two models could be extended to the two probation-promoter countries, namely the United Kingdom and the United States. While American theorists predicted that enforcement might some day overtake rehabilitation and emerge as the primary goal of probation (a change unlikely to occur in the near future), British practices and attitudes appear to go back to the roots, where the tradition of helping the offender is, in turn, unlikely to be easily replaced. In other common law countries, such as Canada or Australia, the relative scarcity of resources offered by the public sector, the concurrent demands for greater accountability in their usage and the public pressure for tougher sanctions pressed the government agencies to adopt correction-oriented strategies.[23]

The same polarity appears between *care* and *control*, two classical functions of probation. Conditional suspension of punishment and supervision of offenders were the original key elements, but their weight alternated in time. Basically, the more emphasis put on the suspension of punishment and the therapeutic aims, the less effective probation is for medium dangerous offenders, and symmetrically, the more emphasis on supervision and restriction of liberty, the higher risk for breaching the required conditions imposed by court. Therefore, in order to accommodate probation with a sentencing framework stressing upon proportionality between punishment and crime, the former has to have a well regulated functional balance.

However, the two functions are complementing each other in practice: supervision involves some form of guidance or treatment, while counseling (casework) and other forms of social work inevitably imply a certain degree of monitoring and control, in order to ensure that the offender actually did notice the requirements of the order.

Theorists suggested several alternatives:

(a) *Separatism*, both organizationally and in daily practice, of the two functions of the probation service. This position has as a premise the inefficiency of social work skills in preventing further offenses. Its supporters emphasized the dissonance between the courts' and the public expectations as to the way probation officers should control offenders, within the existent system in England and Wales, heavily professionalized and having a working ethos firmly grounded in the social work practice.[24] Probation service should, therefore, become a court-based social work service, assisting offenders on an essentially voluntary basis. Some other services, explicitly punitive, should be designed to offer and develop the range of community-based punishments, as alternatives to the damaging effects of the custodial sentences.

(b) *Controlism*, which goes to the opposite direction, by turning the probation service into a *community punishment agency*.[25] The role of the service would be to develop a wider range of punishments in the community. Probation as "control" would be best reflected by an intensive supervision. Accordingly, the classical "advise, assist and befriend" should be replaced with an "advise, assist and compel" philosophy, favorable to an integration of controlism within the just deserts framework.[26] Obviously, by making probation tougher and more effective, controlism may become politically attractive for both conservatives (by cracking down on criminals) and liberals (by keeping a lid on prison population). Used for the first time in the United States,[27] then spread to the United Kingdom,[28] it became the trend of the 1990s. On the other hand, an excessive expansion of the state control may trigger adverse reactions from the rehabilitationist body of the probation services.

(c) Another position, basically separatist, but developing a *balanced service* approach, favored by probation practitioners, goes for a new form of a probation order. The courts would explicitly set supervision and surveillance limits by monitoring the frequency of the reports, while the officers and the probationers would, in turn, voluntarily establish the limits of the social work service. In terms of integration between the functions of control and care, the chief advantages would be a flexibility in probation planning, managing and practice, and a more intense behaviorist approach in examining the realities of probation as they are perceived by probationers.[29] Yet by giving the *social work* component a voluntary basis, the sentence will obviously lose credibility. Besides, leaving the responsibility for asking help to probationers, in the fortunate case where they would have a clear picture about their own difficulties, would reduce the officers' motivation to extend their range of skills.

(d) Probation as *non-treatment*, a "medical model" replacer that would rely upon the officer's unilateral decision rather than on his agreements with the probationer. Stress would be put on community involvement, negotiation, responsibility and an informed choice,[30] meaning volunteering, counseling offenders during supervision and control programming, in accordance with the pre-sentence reports and the probationer's consent.

(e) Probation as a *local community option*, developed in the United States, according to which the mission of probation in America could not be defined nationally but regionally.[31] Yet a discussion at a national level would be useful in order to better define the local options and propose guidelines for choosing a mission. The mission of probation will be defined by the extent and the type of public involvement and the degree to which probation functions would be validated by different communities.

The same *welfare v. justice* dichotomy can be found again in the practice of other countries. In Scotland, Hungary, Israel and Japan, the counseling function is deemed as the core of probation, while control and surveillance are not construed as punitive or correctional in purpose. In Australia, the controlling function has a more central role, with a much greater recognition of the penal or the correctionalist goals. In England and Wales, Canada and Sweden the system is in transition: while counseling (casework) remains a dominant *modus operandi*,[32] the current legislative packages tend to incorporate the community penalties into a coherent desert-based sentencing framework.[33] In England and Wales, government efforts to shift away the balance of probation work from counseling to an intensive supervision encountered the strong resistance of qualified staff, and further managerialist interventions to move the labor force in the correctionalist direction have generated further reluctance.

This overview outlines several conclusions. Probation belongs to the public and the profession, as well, a fact deriving from its functional duality. An excessive stress on one component would be detrimental for the other, activating the traditional conflict of interests between offender and community, and fueling tensions between the government and the qualified staff, though correctionalist trends might be associated with the more bureaucratic or managerialist systems.[34] Politically, the conflict has substantiated the two extreme visions about offenders, viewed by conservatives as a threat to society, and by liberals as victims of an oppressive society. Also, the more goals coupled to its traditional pattern and functions (retribution, rehabilitation, restitution, avoidance of discrimination, reducing recidivism, and crime prevention), the more confusion about the purposes of its component parts.

CHAPTER 7

A HISTORICAL SURVEY

7.1. UNITED KINGDOM

Probation was statutorily established for the first time in the United States but its roots can be found in the earlier English common law schemes of humanizing the criminal justice system.

Mitigation of harsh penalties for young offenders was a practice known in the early Middle Ages. Primitive forms of *indenture* and *binding over with surety for good behavior* for juveniles were found in a decree issued by the Anglo-Saxon king Aethelstan (895-940 A.D.).[1]

An original precedent of probation, practiced in the thirteenth century, was the *benefit of clergy*, applied to clergy members indicted in a King's court, during the reign of Henry II. The offenders, formally under royal court jurisdiction, were in fact subject to the ecclesiastical court authority, more lenient in sentencing and assuring escape from the death penalty. In the fourteenth century, the benefit was extended to other religious ancillaries; in the following centuries it was progressively granted to the secular assistants and the women of the realm, and finally, to all those able to read (although the literacy test was frequently altered by clerks' false statements or by memorization of different passages from the Bible). In 1841, the benefit was abolished by law.[2]

Judicial reprieve (Lat. *reprendere*, to take back), another device for moderating the penalty, consisted in a temporary suspension of sentence,[3] similar in a way to the present-day suspended sentence. Since a new trial or appeal to another court was not sustained in the common law system, reprieve was a fairly widespread practice. Its purpose was to allow a temporary stay, so the defendant might apply to the Crown Court for an absolute or a conditional pardon, or when the judge was dissatisfied with the verdict, the evidence, or the prescribed punishment. This practice, also called *respite*, was employed mostly in the seventeenth century, when the English courts began to grant reprieves to prisoners under sentence of death, on condition that they accept deportation to the colonies (America and then Australia). It was not intended to carry an indefinite suspension of the sentence but prosecution was assumably dropped in many cases, and the suspension became permanent. The device was later taken over by the American courts.

The system of *transportation* to colonies, mentioned above, was another substitute for severe punishment at home and an opportunity for rehabilitation in a new country. The reprivees were permitted to accept transportation and were handed over to contractors, usually shipowners, who engaged to convey them to the colonies. The practice of transportation was suspended in 1847. *The Penal Servitude Act 1857* statutorily recognized the breakdown of the system and introduced the three part sentence: an 18-month confinement with hard labor, a period of public work (but not solitary confinement), and the conditional release, as a ticket-of-leave under Police supervision. The *ticket-of-leave*, an early form of statutory license or parole, was designed to increase the level of supervision. The system was introduced in some colonies (Australia) and then abolished under *The Prison Act 1898*, as a result of the Gladstone Committee Recommendation (1895).[4]

Recognizance (Lat. *recognoscere*, to recall to mind) or the *binding over for good behavior*, a scheme developed under *The Justice of the Peace Act 1361*, is deemed by many as the direct ancestor of probation. Initially, it was a measure of preventive justice, involving an obligation or a promise made under the court order by a person not yet convicted of a crime, that he would "keep the peace" and "be of good behavior." Usually, a *bail* or *sureties* were prerequisites. The surety had the power and the duty to enforce the conditions and return the offender to court in case of breaching the imposed conditions or of reoffending during a specific period. That practice assured good behavior and was extended to individuals convicted of misdemeanors in addition to, or in substitution of, other penalty. *The Criminal Law Consolidation Act 1861* extended recognizance for felons and *The Summary*

Jurisdiction Act 1879 brought amendments which developed the first British probation service. Subsequently, courts created the practice of asking the *police court missionaries* to volunteer in advising and helping recognizees and designing supervision plans.[5]

During the nineteenth century, the English magistrates initiated some experiments of individual social treatment for the young and for first offenders, in order to avoid the prison stigma. In the early 1820, a Warwick County magistrate passed a token sentence of 1-day imprisonment for a young offender upon the condition that the offender would return to parental care or to his master's supervision.[6] In 1841, Matthew Davenport Hill, Recorder of Birmingham, employed a *Magistrates Bail* system to suspend a sentence and release the offender to "suitable guardians" from a list of voluntary helpers. Hill used the word *probationer* and treated very severely such offenders if later convicted of further offenses; also, he arranged with the Chief Superintendent of Police for "a confidential officer" to visit the guardian and to keep a record of their findings. After 17 years of experience (1841-1858), he reported a 16% reconviction rate (78 offenders of a total of 483 released at the Birmingham Sessions).[7] *The Criminal Law Consolidation Act 1861* statutorily confirmed the common law practice of giving to courts the power to release offenders on recognizance. In the 1870s, another judge, Edward William Cox, Recorder of Portsmouth, used recognizance as a punishment substitute, hiring a special "inquiry officer" to supervise the behavior of the released, a practice favorably received by the Home Office and the general public.[8] The experiments of Hill and Cox led the way to the adoption of probation at a later date.

In the second half of the nineteenth century, drunkenness and alcohol abuse, stimulated by unemployment, poverty and precarious housing conditions, were social problems of particular concern in big cities. People were frequently brought before the criminal courts and sent to prison for drunkenness and other related offenses. In August 1876, the Church of England Temperance Society,[9] at the initiative of Frederick Rainer, a Hertfordshire printer, appointed in London the first unpaid police court missionary, followed by other appointments, so that by 1900 a number of 143 employed missionaries, sponsored by a range of religious charities, formed what had become known as the police court mission. Their task was to make inquiries into the background of people who appeared before the court and, if the court agreed, to accept responsibility for the offender's care and supervision. Sometimes they provided money for bails, made matrimonial conciliation, assisted difficult children and were involved in the voluntary care of prisoners on release. The precursors of today's probation officers were two police court missionaries, George Nelson and William Batchelor, ex-Coldstream Guardsmen, whose aim was basically an evangelical one: to reclaim the lives and souls of drunkards who appeared before the courts; they were asking the magistrates to bind individuals over into their care and were undertaking to secure their "restoration and reclamation."[10] Serving without an official authority, and working often against opposition, the missionaries won the confidence of the magistrates and the public. At a time in Boston (Massachusetts), where *The Probation Act 1878* was already regulating the appointment of the "probation officers," the Howard Association, a penal reform group in Britain, willing to capitalize on the American experience, acted like a pressure group in trying to reform the British system. A year later, *The Summary Jurisdiction Act 1879*, improperly claimed by some as being a probation law, stated that trivial offenders should be conditionally discharged with no punishment, on giving security to appear for sentence, if called upon. *The Probation of First Offenders Act 1887* provided that the first offenders found guilty of more serious offenses and originally proposed for statutory supervision should be released on recognizance, but this amendment was ruled out in Parliament. This was a first step for an authorized offender supervision.

The credibility of the new system, built up by police court missionaries, facilitated the adoption of *The Probation of Offenders Act 1907* and of the first *Probation Rules*, which allowed local authorities to appoint in January 1908 probation officers whose job was to supervise offenders. According to the 1907 Act, the probation officers had to "advise, assist and befriend" people under supervision, a principle almost unaltered to the present day. Since the probationer was to be under the supervision of a named person, personal links between him and the officer were deemed as very important. Probation officers were appointed by the magistrates' courts and paid by the local authorities. Gradually, from missionaries of a voluntary body, they turned into secular social workers of the court. In 1925, a new criminal justice act set the standard administrative framework for probation service, which became mandatory for every court petty session division. *The Criminal*

Justice Act 1925, amended by *The Criminal Justice Amendment Act 1926*, established probation service as statutory, that is a state-provided and a state-funded service. *The Criminal Justice Act 1948* outlined the general framework for the organization and procedure of the current system. Recognizance in probation orders was replaced with simple orders requiring the offender, with his consent if 14 or over, to be under a 1-to-3-year supervision. Also, the officer's name was to be replaced with the petty session division which the officer belonged to.[11]

In 1959, the Home Office appointed a Departmental Committee on the Probation Service, headed by R. P. Morison. The committee reviewed the activity of the probation service and approved development guidelines, issuing a report finalized in 1962. Probation was defined as being the offender's submission, while at liberty, to a specified period of supervision done by a social caseworker (an improper term for the probation officer), who was an officer of the court. The offender was held liable during the supervision period and sent to court, in case of bad conduct.[12] Dealing with the offender's needs was considered a task of the welfare state, and accordingly, probation officers were encouraged to establish relationships that would positively influence their clients' behavior. The report encouraged the expansion of probation service and proposed extensive prerogatives of the adult offender after-care. In 1965, the Probation Service became the Probation and After-Care Service.

The 1950s and the early 1960s were the culmination of the *treatment era*, and the rehabilitative ideal achieved its consummation in *The Children and Young Persons Act 1969*. The 1969 Act kept the original wording of the "advise, assist and befriend" (introduced by the 1907 Act), but the issue of *care vs. control* was to be a dominant subject in the following years. The Act brought also some novelties, such as the *supervision order*, designed for teens under 17, and the *intermediate treatment*, for juveniles. *Community service*, *day training centers* and *adult probation hostels* were to be regulated by statutes in 1972 and 1973.

Another significant event of the period was *The Social Work (Scotland) Act 1968*, which disbanded the Scottish Probation Service and abolished the title of probation officer. The welfare, child-care and probation services were integrated into joint local authority social-work departments, and the juvenile courts were replaced by a system of *children's hearings*. All these changes were aimed to avoid overlapping between various services whose prerogatives in the community were substantially resembling. The Scottish Act triggered long debates in England and Wales about the future of the probation service. Eventually, the probation service kept its autonomy, while the welfare and the child-care services merged into some new social-services departments of local subordination. The main reasons were the close and special relationship between courts and the probation service, and the desire to keep the decision-making process related to offenders at a national level, allegedly more consistent than the various local influences.[13]

In the 1970s, probation service responsibilities were extended to the supervision of multiple serious offenders, as a result of the Government's desire to decrease the prison population and thereby save money. To that extent, *The Powers of Criminal Courts Act 1973* introduced *community service* for offenders aged 17 or over, as a reparative measure of performing unpaid work for the community. Under the new circumstances, the probation service had to supervise a larger number of offenders, many of them deserving perhaps custodial sentences. The new task was assumed with reluctance. Ten years later, *The Criminal Justice Act 1982* expanded the set of requirements and activities for the *day centers* and returned the original name of the service, namely the Probation Service, without the After-Care component. In time, the number of the released persons subject to statutory supervision increased constantly. Nevertheless, the probation officer, whose caseload used to cover a wide range of individual needs and problems, turned out to be a Home Office representative, in charge of organizing and providing additional sentencing resources.[14] Such a situation was partly the effect of criminological labeling theories and the radical sociologists' critiques, dominant in the epoch, which undermined the *casework ideology*. Also, Martison's 1974 research and its ultrapessimistic results as to efficacy of treatment,[15] were echoed by a series of Home Office IMPACT studies on reconviction rates made in the same period.[16] Although their conclusions were labeled as unconvincing (e.g., the experiments were repeated after too short a period of time, i.e. one year, instead of longer periods),[17] confidence in the *treatment programs* was obviously weakened. Some even prognosticated the end of the probation era.[18] But the late 1980s and the early 1990s brought a more hopeful picture. New research found out that working with persistent offenders and using social work interventions, such as intensive groupworks, would lessen reconviction rates after periods longer than 1 year.[19]

7.2. UNITED STATES OF AMERICA

In America, probation was already having precedents a long time before the term as such was coined by John Augustus in the early 1840s. In the late eighteenth century, colonial jails and correctional houses were set up after the English pattern and were equally repressive. In 1790, Pennsylvania adopted a system of solitary confinement, under Quaker influence, taken over by other state prisons. In 1815, Massachusetts enforced severe rule of discipline in the state prisons, which affected human dignity. There were some pressing groups advocating for a more humane treatment in prison, like The Boston Prison Discipline Society, established in 1826,[20] but there were also earlier accounts about more lenient devices applicable to individual cases. For instance, *release on bail for good behavior* was practiced by the colonial Massachusetts courts since the seventeenth century,[21] and the *benefit of clergy* was frequently used in the seventeenth and the eighteenth centuries.[22]

Judicial reprieve played an important role in the evolution of probation in America. Whereas the English courts never intended to use the reprieve as an indefinite suspension of sentence, in America the device became a precedent for some courts after granting suspension of sentence, as long as the defendant behaved himself. Some state courts viewed it as a common law device, but most of the states regulated reprieve by statutes before the emergence of the first probation acts.[23]

Another ancestor of probation was the *provisional "filing" of cases*, practiced by the Massachusetts courts in the nineteenth century.[24] The court was able to suspend the imposition of sentence, under certain requirements, when extenuating circumstances were discovered during trial, after the verdict of guilt but before the imposition of sentence. The order was not replacing the final judgment, and sentencing could be revived by court upon motion of either party.

Recognizance, with or without *sureties*, was practiced in seventeenth century colonial America in a similar manner as in England. Massachusetts continued to use release on recognizance with sureties during the eighteenth and the early nineteenth centuries. In the nineteenth century, the device was applied frequently in all of New England, mostly to young and petty offenders, when imprisonment was not considered as suitable. Apparently, the first use of recognizance was reported in the case of *Commonwealth vs. Chase* (1830), tried by the Municipal Court of Boston.[25] The device was extensively and imaginatively used in years to come. In 1836, Massachusetts passed for the first time a bill, subsequently amended in 1865 and 1869,[26] authorizing recognizance with sureties at any stage of trial, insofar as it applied to petty offenders in the lower courts. The lawmaker intended to ensure a law-abiding behavior for a specific period of time after sureties had been pledged by friends.

The device of sureties, or *bail*, was employed either with or without simultaneously binding over the offender on his own recognizance. Bail as such (when not combined with recognizance), a device for the temporary suspension of the punishment, also had a major historical significance for the evolution of some rudimentary practices of probation.

John Augustus (1785-1859), respected as the "father of probation," is credited with originating the modern concept of this non-custodial sanction. In 1841, as a private citizen, he began to supervise offenders released to his custody by the Police Court of Boston. His initiative was obviously influenced by social movements of the time, already in progress, like the abolition of slavery, the campaign for women's rights and the temperance crusade. Like other early reformers, Augustus was also motivated by a religious concern for saving people on the fringes of society, like drunkards, beggars, prostitutes and vagrant children, from their sins. According to middle-class morality, getting those persons on bail meant the use of a strict discipline, in order to put them on the "right path."[27] In the following eighteen years, he closely supervised 1,946 male and female adults, and several thousands of children and teens, helping them get jobs and establish themselves in the community. Augustus identified the alleged redeemable persons by using rudimentary techniques of selection (age, character, work habits); then he made a recommendation to the court that probation be granted. He also developed conditions for probation (mostly work requirements), and supervised his clients for a period usually limited to thirty days.

Between 1859 (Augustus' death) and 1878, probation work was voluntarily undertaken by individuals and agencies.[28] Augustus' work inspired the Massachusetts legislators to pass the 1878 act, which outlined the classical probation with supervision as an alternative to imprisonment and authorized the appointment of a probation officer in Boston, paid by the Suffolk County municipality. In 1880, probation was extended to other Massachusetts counties, and by 1898 it already spread to the superior (felony) courts.[29] Other states copied the Massachusetts experience, either by producing versions of the 1887 English "probation" (without supervision) or by limiting the alternative to certain categories of offenders, such as the 1887 Missouri Parole Act (with no supervision), the 1894 Maryland Act ("release on probation" with no supervision), the 1898 Vermont Act (probation after the suspension of the imposition of sentence), the 1899 Rhode Island Act (probation before the conviction or imposition of sentence, but limited to petty offenses), the 1899 Minnesota and Illinois Acts (probation for juveniles). In 1925, the federal government designed a juvenile probation system for the U.S. district courts. As for adult probation, it was not before 1956 when such a system was available in each state.[30] This slow development can be explained by the public feeling toward community sentences, less strong in America than in England. Also, because hundreds of U.S. agencies were operating under different state regulations, a coherent philosophy about probation was often seen as a very difficult task to perform. Some states were having agencies profiled on certain types of offenders, while others were having separate agencies for all types of offenders. *The Sentencing Reform Act 1984* limited somewhat the inconsistency in the sentencing process caused by traditional court discretion, by fixing minimum custodial terms through "mandatory minimum" sentences. Critics viewed these efforts as inefficient and as affecting the poor.[31] Nonetheless, probation has gradually imposed itself as the most widely used correctional mechanism in the United States.

7.3. THE BRITISH COMMONWEALTH

7.3.1. CANADA. The early pre-statutory probation devices have developed in a flexible common law jurisdiction that allowed the existent practices to gradually adjust to new needs and objectives. The Canadian judiciary inherited British conservatism and did not overstep its common law prerogatives, unlike the United States, where the authorities revised the original legal status of such devices.[32] In the late 1880s, the young offenders were usually released on *recognizance* with or without *sureties* on specific terms. First offenders committing 2-year imprisonment offenses were usually put on *conditional release*. In 1892, *probation* was regulated by the Criminal Code, and *The Ontario Juvenile Probation Act 1893* appointed volunteers from children's agencies as supervisors. The Criminal Code was amended in 1921 with provisions related to breach proceedings, the sentencing options of restitution and reparation, and the obligation for families to pay for the offender's maintenance. In 1956, a Royal Commission recommended that eligibility for probation should be extended to all offenders, except the serious ones. The recommendation was enforced by statutes in 1967 and 1970; also, the acts outlined a new framework for breaches.[33]

The slow developing of probation and the process of redefining its identity in a rather correctional than a therapeutic framework, with a tight managerial control, are features that get the Canadian system closer to the Australian one. Also, its positioning within a "tariff" system of penalties shows a transit from the common law to the statute law, a tendency which has already become obvious in England.

7.3.2. AUSTRALIA. As already mentioned, in the eighteenth and the nineteenth centuries, the most efficient method to avoid prison overcrowding in England was the system of *transporting* the offenders to colonies. It was practical (less criminals in a country lacking at the time coherent rehabilitation programs) and profitable, both for the colonial administration (cheap labor force) and the shipping companies (regular transportation of convicts packed off in great numbers).

Initially, England sent about 2,000 convicts to her American colonies, but soon after the 1776 American Declaration of Independence and the English-American war that followed, transportation of criminals was shifted to the newly discovered Territories in the South Seas. In the last quarter of the eighteenth century, over 15,000 men and women were shipped to New South Wales alone.[34] On arrival, the prisoners were lodged in isolated, and often uncoordinated, correctional camps, or employed in convict gangs on public work. Later, as their number grew, they were bound out to anyone interested in employing them. In the 1840s, the stream of convicts was directed to Tasmania. There, the convicts with good conduct were granted conditional liberty, usually through *tickets-of-leave*.[35] This was a primitive form of probation, with no coherent plan to reform the individual, nor any treatment, guidance or supervision. In fact, Australian probation was lacking the strong Christian component the English and American versions used to have, which explains its subsequent evolution as a rather correctional than a voluntary or philanthropic activity. *The New South Wales Prisons Act 1840* laid the basis for incarceration having both deterrent and reformatory aspects and outlined the correctionalist system which prevailed in the following century. In 1886, Queensland experimented with the French version of probation (the 1884 Berenger bill). South Australia passed bills regulating devices such as conditional release for first offenders (1887), probation for juveniles (1895) and adult offenders (1913), where, unlike their English duplicates, only the imposition of sentence was suspended. New South Wales passed a similar bill in 1924.

Probation developed slowly, due to the tremendous distance between Australia and England. It may be considered rather a postwar phenomenon, in spite of a relatively well-organized juvenile system.[36] In the 1950s, New South Wales and South Australia each established adult probation services under state prison departments (in 1951 and 1954, respectively).

Basically, the Australian sentencing philosophy maintained, with some variations in time, its correctionalist character, according to which helping the offender should not be detrimental to the society protection. In the short run, this goal is to be achieved through surveillance and monitoring, and in the long run, by counseling and educational programs.

7.3.3. NEW ZEALAND. Statutory probation was preceded by *release on recognizance*, practiced as a suspension of the imposition of the sentence for good behavior. The first probation bill was enacted in 1886, following the American pattern (stress on supervision) and distancing itself from the 1887 English Act. The first successful experiments in Massachusetts stimulated the local lawmakers to adopt probation (eligibility for first offenders, like in England, and optional recognizance for good behavior) and design a specialized service (officers with a fixed salary, appointed by the Governor, in charge with offender supervision and the in-court report-making.[37] *The Offenders Probation Act 1920* extended the criteria of eligibility and the officers' prerogatives related to supervision and employment arrangements. The National Probation Service, founded in the 1950s, had its officers appointed by the Minister of Justice. *The Criminal Justice Act 1985* set up a centralized probation service, as part of the community correction service, and empowered the probation officers, in addition to classical supervision, to refer the offenders to the community-based organizations.[38]

7.3.4. OTHER COUNTRIES. In South Africa, *conditional release* for the first offenders was enacted in the late nineteenth century, and a rudimentary form of supervision was carried out by the police.[39] Subsequent statutes stipulated a general eligibility for *probation*, except for serious offenders, and an extended supervision for adult offenders. Because of a lack of full-time staff, stress was put on volunteering.

In India, *probation* was enforced by the 1923 and the 1931 acts, mostly for juvenile delinquents. Traditional community played an important role as to the life of the individual and facilitated the spread of rehabilitative ideals. Following a 1934 initiative, the federal government extended the probation service network to the state level: in 1936, in Madras (Madhya Pradesh), then in 1938, in Bombay (Uttar Pradesh). *The Probation of Offenders Act 1958* imposed more accurate standards for state law. In the 1970s, 20 out of the 25 states attuned their legislation with the national standards. Yet probation developed slowly due to insufficient material and financial resources and, equally, to the absence of a political will able to shape a more coherent and unitary strategy in the field.[40]

CHAPTER 8

CURRENT TRENDS
IN THE UNITED KINGDOM

In past decades, the evolution of probation was indissolubly linked with the political orientations of the time.

In the United Kingdom, the Conservative administration (1979-1997) favored a shift of focus, away from a welfare state that provided a safety net for all, to a system where greater emphasis was laid on market forces.[1] *Penal protectionism* prevailed in the society-offender relationship, which resulted in higher imprisonment rates and a higher centralized control of the defensive units (among them, the probation service). For instance, the 1985 criminal statistics showed that the areas with the highest imprisonment rates were run by Tories, while the ones with the lowest rates were run by Labors.[2] The conclusion should not be deemed as an axiom, particularly because courts cannot be equated with political parties, but the fact as such stands. A year before, the Home Office published a *Statement of National Objectives and Priorities* for the probation service, setting out how the Government viewed at the time the work parameters of the service and how it looked toward a possible future development. In fact, the document created widespread concern, since it foresaw a new stage of more centralized control and privatization. Critics viewed the more intensified institutionalization of community service as leading to an underestimation of the after-care work with offenders released from custody and of the civil work done by the service.[3] In 1990, the government green paper *Supervision and Punishment in the Community* argued, on the contrary, that a more centralized control of probation service would be a prerequisite for a more efficient and standardized service countrywide.[4] In the same year, the government white paper *Crime, Justice and Protecting the Public* outlined the aims of offender supervision, namely the public protection, the prevention against reoffending, and a successful reintegration of the offender back into the community. What seemed obvious for many was that *the client*, the intended beneficiary of the probation officer's interventions, was not the probationer, but the community.[5] Nevertheless, the government U-turn was an understandable reaction toward the increasing number of probation orders granted to offenders who served previous custodial sentences.[6] There was also a general attempt to standardize the good practice. National standards emerged in April 1989, and several drafts on topics affecting probation service were circulated and commented on by August 1992.[7] The final versions of seven National Standards were eventually published in August 1992, and they covered areas of work related to pre-sentence reports, probation orders, supervision orders, community service orders, combination orders, management of hostels, and supervision before and after the release from custody.[8]

The standards became operational when most of *The Criminal Justice Act 1991* provisions entered into force. The act changed significantly the community penalty structure, its range, terminology and philosophy. The Home Office vision was to offer a "new sentencing framework" where sentences would reflect the seriousness of the offense, and custody should apply only to the violent and to sex offenders ("the custody threshold," *CJA 1991*, s. 1). That was a clear intention to install proportionality as the leading rationale for sentencing, though concepts as *just desert* or *retribution* were not mentioned. A direct consequence was that community orders became community sentences, and the label of "alternatives to custody" given to community orders in the past disappeared. A probation order was no longer imposed "instead of sentencing" but became a court sentence in its own right. In other words, there was no legal obstacle to combining the new "penalties" with other penalties, financial or community-based, as part of a community sentence. Nevertheless, the condition to obtain the offender's consent was not removed. But control and surveillance became predominant in the detriment of the rehabilitative ideals, and the legislation was speaking of an "offender" rather than a "probationer." The minimum age for a probationer was lowered from 17 to 16 years. However, as *The CJA 1991*, s. 6(2) put it, the restrictions on liberty must be "commensurate with the seriousness of the offense" and the order should be "the most suitable for the offender," an attempt to combine proportionality with individualization.[9] Probation officers, as "officers of the court," were held responsible for a larger number of reports to the court than in the past. The pre-sentence reports were given a key role in collecting information and in the sentencing; except the offenses triable on indictment, there the court must obtain and consider a pre-sentence report before holding its decision. The reports should include proposals on how the offender can be dealt with if given a community sentence. For the first time, *The CJA 1991*, s. 95 imposed on the staff the obligation to avoid discriminatory practices. In the first few months after the enforcement, the number of probation orders fell significantly, especially for young offenders aged 16-20 sentenced for theft (50%) and burglary (30%). The combination order, newly introduced, had similar trends, while the community service orders grew, as before, but at a slower rate.[10]

In April 1992, Home Office, supplier of 80% of the probation service funds, imposed "cash limiting," holding tighter sway over budgets; in November, it designed a series of 3-year plans in order to shape a cost-effective service, viewed as a "value for money" provider, characterized by "efficiency and effectiveness," and an "effective program" promoter in a safe supervision of offenders in the community.[11]

The subsequent statutes hardened the government orientation initiated in the 1980s. Thus, *The Criminal Justice Act 1993* abolished the "two offense rule," applicable to community sentences. Previously, the court could look at the combined seriousness of two concurrent offenses, when deciding whether the offense was serious enough to warrant a community sentence; according to the 1993 Act, it should look at the combined seriousness of all concurrent offenses. The rule was also applied to custodial sentences; *The CJA 1993*, s. 66(4). The change caused a certain anxiety for it could allegedly lead to a harsher sanctioning of minor offenses.[12] Also, *The Criminal Justice and Public Order Act 1994*, Schedule 9, par. 40, abolished the mandatory character of the pre-sentence reports for the court due to the high rate of court adjournments made to obtain reports even when they were having a minimum impact on the sentencing outcome.[13] Nonetheless, the level of pre-sentence reports remained constantly high, while the number of probation orders keeps on growing.[14] The protectionist and efficientist policy reached its heights when the Tory government enforced *The National Standards 1995*. The Standards were preceded by a September 1994 revised draft, issued on 9 March 1995.[15] By far, the standards in their latest version exceeded the value of a mere recommendation by "imposing" a rather statutory language.[16] Public protection and crime impact upon victims were set as top priorities. More rigorous programs were designed to supervise offenders in the community, and the work done by officers and service managers became more specialized (supervision for different types of offenders, specialized teams in the community service, Crown Courts, family courts, through-care and after-care).

The government green paper *Strengthening Punishment in the Community* (March 1995) marked a new stage in the evolution of probation, comparable with *The CJA 1991*. The document goes for a revised structure of community sentences, able to give the courts more flexibility in determining their content. The post-1991 practice revealed that courts had some difficulties applying the principles of proportionality to community sentences. Apparently, probation and supervision orders were not offering sufficient punishment, while community service orders were not expressly aimed at preventing further offending. Those shortcomings were to be overcome by a single integrated community sentence, "incorporating and extending" the current range of community orders.[17] Supposedly, the new community sentence would give the courts greater liberty in combining the components of the existing community orders and a greater certainty that the supervision plan would be implemented in a particular way. This view was sustained by research findings suggesting that supervision programs could have a higher impact in preventing recidivism if they would be clearly structured at the outset, involved in directed work and carried out as planned. The offender's consent in court for issuing a community sentence was regarded as superfluous, given the option between a community penalty and custody, and was to be abolished.

The basics of the new order, termed the *community sentence*, would consist in the restriction of liberty, reparation, and prevention of reoffending. *Restriction of liberty* could be met with a curfew, an attendance center order, a certain number of hours of community service, probation supervision involving some restriction of liberty, attending or forgoing specified activities, or any combination of these forms. *Reparation* would take the form of either a compensation to individual victims or the unpaid work for the benefit of the community, or both. Finally, *prevention of reoffending* would be substantiated by program packages, ranging from the very intensive and covering the full maximum 3 years of supervision permitted, to the short and specific (alcohol education, offense-focused group works, various forms of training designed to improve employability).[18]

Yet some issues were left open to debate. For instance, there was no indication as to which category of offenders and offenses the new order was designed for, how suitable the three-element set might be for a specific offender keeping the 1991 Act standards, or how such a "cocktail" sentence will impact the breaching rate. If these proposals are to be incorporated in a statute, it is highly probable that courts would require further guiding elements, in order to avoid too large a room for eclectic practices.

The new Labor administration, in power since May 1997, will probably attempt to redesign the probation service within its classical rehabilitationist coordinates. Still this will definitely not be an easy task after almost two decades of Tory correctionalist philosophy, constantly promoted in statutory law.

CHAPTER 9

REQUIREMENTS

9.1. ELIGIBILITY

Before passing any probation order or other community sentence, the court must be satisfied that the offense or the concurrent offenses are serious enough to warrant this; *CJA 1991*, s. 6(1). The seriousness of an offense is assessed on the basis of all relevant information (pre-sentence report data, the aggravating and the mitigating factors, etc.). The probation officer's recommendation plays a key role in the court's final decision. In over 75% of the cases, the final decision followed the conclusions of the recommendations (80% in England,[1] 95% in the United States[2]). There is no absolute standard of seriousness warranting a probation order but it is a matter of fact and judgment for the court. The lack of a tariff system which hierarchically sets the community sentences, facilitated the use of individual orders or the combined orders for offenses with different degrees of seriousness. The courts assess gravity by taking into account the offender's previous criminal record and his failures to respond to previous sentences, if any; *CJA 1991*, s. 29(1), as amended by *CJA 1993*, s. 66(6). Courts should clearly identify which previous convictions or failures are relevant and then consider the effect of such convictions or failures in relation to seriousness, otherwise the severity of a punishment would automatically be higher than in the previous sentence.[3] A further developing of proper instruments able to identify the "dangerous" offender is deemed as desirable, especially when the seriousness of the offense frequently overshadows other sentencing criteria, such as the offender's personality.[4] Tough or lenient policies, practiced by different courts and probation departments may be totally unrelated to the needs of the individual offender and may offer no realistic protection to society.[5] Preliminary investigations and pre-sentence reports are frequently reduced to filling in forms and grounding the recommendation on the number of offenses committed. But a satisfactory determination of *dangerousness* for legal purposes is a very difficult, if not impossible, task.

The legal criteria for dangerousness, far from being simple predictions, are assessments taking the form of predictive judgments. They do not merely refer to the likeliness that a certain individual will commit a further offense. Rather, they make thorough evaluations of the concrete circumstances in which the offense was committed and of the offender's personality, in order to detect inclinations to adopt a similar behavior in similar circumstances in the future.

In the 1950s and the 1960s, U.S. researchers attempted to distinguish high-risk offenders from other offenders. A serious obstacle was the low frequency of repeating serious offenses by the high-risk offenders, which created "false positive" errors of prediction.[6] Although errors were "diluted" by enlarging the percentage of serious offenders in samples, this type of research still could not make "just" predictive judgments for sentencing purposes. This task was taken over by "case studies," made on an individual basis.

In the 1970s, research indicated a high proportion of agreement between psychiatric recommendations and court evaluations (86.7%) and a strong link between the seriousness of the offense and the offender's dangerousness (75% of those serious offenses were reported dangerous).[7]

In the 1980s, the *risk prediction scales* became frequently used by American probation departments. The scales were closely related to the evolution of intensive supervision programs, due to a series of factors. First, at this time probation was deemed to be the ideal solution for massive prison overcrowding, a very stressful factor for the staff. Secondly, successive budget cuts at the correction departments amplified some efficientist trends to limit the needs under the allocated resources and to document further needs when requesting additional funds.[8] Eventually, from a device designed to provide a second chance for young and petty offenders, probation turned itself into a means of reducing the pressures of an overcrowded and underfunded correctional system. In that context, the community supervision of potentially dangerous offenders became crucial in the eligibility process. Statistical data showed that, far from being used for minor or first offenders, probation was granted for about 25% of serious offenders.[9] Furthermore, probation officers were put in charge of supervising other categories of serious offenders released from custody, such as young and adult parolees, life licensees, and persons discharged from psychiatric hospitals. These economic grounds were completed, both in the United Kingdom and the United States, with the arsenal of the rehabilitationist philosophy, according to which the high-risk offenders "are not, however, dangerous," that "they differ from other people by virtue of their offense only" and that "to label someone as being dangerous can be very misleading," so an effective supervision would be perfectly possible if done by experienced officers.[10] The boomerang effect of reoffending which followed later placed probation under siege. The toughest attacks were coming from those denouncing the gaps of supervision, but otherwise, critics tried to be as effective as possible. On one hand, it became obvious that supervision and control in the community had some flaws. Many research studies painted the long-term probation effectiveness in preventing recidivism as an overwhelmingly negative one. On the other hand, supervision, in spite of its low impact in the long run upon recidivism, appeared to postpone reconviction while in force,[11] proving itself more useful for protective rather than rehabilitative purposes. Yet the length of delay in committing a further offense remained unknown, since the effect has only been demonstrated in relation to fairly short-term supervision,[12] however atypical for dangerous offenders. There is still much to be done in assessing effectiveness of supervision on different categories of offenses and offenders. It was confirmed though a direct relationship between probation violation rates and the number of previous convictions.[13] Usually, supervision varies with the offenders' personality and the types of offenses they commit, so what is deemed as protective for some can be ineffective for others. However, a lesser use of prison, if practiced, should be compensated with more control in the community. In those cases where serious offenders are to be released into the community, the transcript of the trial should be made available to the supervising probation officers. In many cases, this might be the only solid evidence about the circumstances in which the offense was committed and the potential trigger factors for further offenses. Preferably, the supervision team should include a supervising officer, a senior probation officer, a local assistant chief probation officer, and any other person deemed as relevant, for instance a medical officer for restriction orders, or a warden if the probationer resides in a hostel. Likewise, the special training programs for staff should be focused on knowledge, personal skills and testing of psychological aptitudes.[14]

The risk prediction scales tested the relationship between the risk of reoffending and the offender's need for help (in the United States, the Wisconsin model),[15] or between the gravity of an offense and the offender's criminal history (in the United Kingdom, the Cambridgeshire risk of custody scale and the Staffordshire sentencing prediction scale).[16] Broadly, complete information about the offender's background is paramount for an effective supervision in the community, but not all the time are probation officers informed about the circumstances in which a serious offense was committed. The real personality of an offender can be more accurately pictured by various social inquiry reports compiled from the court decisions, the police briefs on criminal records, or the case-notes made by the prison probation officers and other officials.

9.2. CONDITIONS

In England and Wales, a probation order can be made on any offender aged 16 years or over, for a period between 6 months and 3 years. Every probation order requires the offender to be under the supervision of a probation officer or social worker,[17] but the court can add into the order any requirement deemed as necessary in order to secure good behavior and prevention again recidivism. The *standard conditions*, which courts traditionally include in the orders, are non-statutory in nature, meaning non-compulsory, and therefore they are not affected by the legislation in force. They require the probationer to maintain good behavior and lead an industrious life, inform immediately the probation officer of any change in residence or employment, report periodically and receive the officer's visits at home.[18] Some superior courts omit the clauses of "good behavior" and "industrious life," regarded as no longer appropriate, since nowadays many probationers are unable to find work. Supervision is regarded as ineffective in the case of an offender who is about to leave the country or be drafted, and issuing a probation order in these circumstances is viewed as inopportune.[19]

The court may also include *specific conditions* for part of or for the full duration of the order, in order to secure rehabilitation, protection of the public and prevention against recidivism. In particular, a probation order may not require the offender to pay a monetary compensation for loss, damage or injury caused by his offense. In such cases, a compensation order made in addition to a probation order is the appropriate course, but failure to make payments under such an order cannot amount to a breach of the probation order. *The Powers of Criminal Courts Act 1973* (Sch. 1A), as amended by *The Criminal Justice Act 1991* (s. 9) have set out five types of additional requirements, related to: residence, activities, attending a probation center, treatment for mental condition, and treatment for drug or alcohol dependency, with special reference to sex offenders.

Requirement of residence is imposed after considering the offender's initial residence and surroundings, information usually available from the pre-sentence report. Courts are not precluded to make general residential requirements, although a specific requirement amending the order is viewed as a more reasonable solution. Usually, residential requirements refer to approved probation hostels,[20] private houses,[21] or even non-approved institutions,[22] but the court cannot require a probationer to live where supervision would be ineffective.[23]

Courts have the statutory power to require probationers to participate or to refrain from participating in *specified activities* indicated in the order, and to report to a specified person, at a specified place, for periods not exceeding 60 days. This condition encourages the participation of probationers in different programs and activities organized by the probation service. The range of these programs varies, but one particular activity is statutorily provided, that is the *day center*. Probationers can be required to attend a day center for a period of maximum 60 days. *The CJA 1991* (Sch. 1A, par. 3) renamed the day centers as *probation centers*, in order to use a uniform standard for all facilities and to better reflect their evening activities.[24]

Requirements may also refer to a *treatment for mental condition*, extendible for part of or for the full duration of the order, under the supervision of a qualified medical practitioner. If the probationer resides or is about to reside abroad, he may be required by court to follow the treatment in the respective country. The probation officer is relieved to exercise daily supervision if the probationer is in treatment as a resident patient, but this does not preclude friendly contacts with him, in cooperation with the doctor. The officer remains responsible for discharge or amendment of the order and will normally keep in touch with the probationer's family to prepare for his return; *PCCA 1973*, Sch. 1A, par. 5, and the *Probation Rules 1965*, r. 35(3).

The *treatment for drug or alcohol dependency* may be included when the court assesses that the dependency caused or contributed to the committing of the offense. Before *The CJA 1991*, arrangements for such a treatment were made informally; the probation services used to inform the court of the availability of local facilities and the court usually included the requirement when viewed as appropriate. The requirement was provided for the first time by *The PCCA 1973* (Sch. 1A, par. 6), in a similar manner with the mental treatment. It is deemed as compulsory only if a duly qualified person (a medical practitioner or a person with experience in working with the addicted) is able to provide a suitable treatment of a high standard. The treatment may be either residential or non-residential, at an institution or under supervision, as specified.

Requirements for sex offenders impose participation in specific activities or in probation centers, with no time limitations, which means they are extendible for the full duration of the order; *PCCA 1973*, Sch. 1A, par. 4. The current provisions encourage the courts to deal with sex offenders, where appropriate, by a closer supervision in the community rather than by imprisonment, and in doing so they have important implications for the probation service as to its functions to reduce the risk of reoffending and to protect the public.

The National Standards 1995 recommended that the first meeting between the probation officer and the probationer should take place within 5 working days after the order was issued and be arranged before the probationer leave the court, if possible. At the first meeting, the probationer should be given written information about the requirements of being on probation and the consequences for breaching the order, meaning the execution of penalty in custody.[25]

In Scotland, the current statutes[26] provide probation as an order, not as a sentence (like in England and Wales), meaning that it is considered an alternative to the execution of punishment, not a punishment in its own right.

Probation orders apply to offenders aged 18 or over, and sometimes to minors under 16. Supervision is carried out by personnel from the social work department. The court must obtain and consider a social inquiry report prepared by the social worker of the local authority before making a probation order, disposing an offender under 16 or one subject to a supervision requirement imposed by a children's hearing. For this purpose, it may adjourn the case for maximum a 21 days. The standard probation order requires the offender to be of good behavior and to conform to the directions of the supervising social worker, who will advise and guide him, and periodically visit him at home. A probation order may also require the probationer to: pay compensation to the victim (unlike in England and Wales), undergo a psychological or a psychiatric treatment, live at a specified place, undertake unpaid work for the benefit of the community, attend intensive training programs or carry on other rehabilitating activities.[27] Before the enforcement of *The CJA 1991*, transfer of probationers of 16 and 17 years old from Scotland to England and Wales was difficult, since the former Scottish *juvenile courts* were not empowered to make probation orders for them. The 1991 Act replaced the juvenile courts with the *youth courts*, empowered them to make probation and supervision orders for offenders under 18, and made new arrangements for transferring such orders from Scotland to England; *The Criminal Procedure (Scotland) Act 1975*, ss. 183 and 384, as amended by *CJA 1991*, Sch. 3, part II. Youth courts can supervise probation orders made in Scotland and make supervision orders in lieu of the Scottish probation orders.

In Northern Ireland, probation orders are still regulated by *The Probation Act (Northern Ireland) 1950*, as amended. *The CJA 1991* provisions related to the community orders are not applicable, as in Scotland, but currently the local legislation is under review, in order to adjust itself to the new changes of the past decades. Juveniles are supervised under probation orders for a period between 6 months and 3 years, not supervision orders (as in England and Wales), unless the court specifically decides that the local authority should supervise them. During that period the juvenile has to lead an honest and industrious life. According to the *Treatment of Offenders (Northern Ireland) Order 1989,* the court may impose further conditions to the order, e.g., attending at a specified place for a period of maximum 60 days. The court must resort to a different penalty if the juvenile aged 14 to 16 does not have to be placed on probation. The adult offenders are supervised by probation officers. Probation orders made in England and Wales may be carried out in Scotland and Northern Ireland, according to a procedure established by *The CJA 1991* (Sch. 3, pars. 1 and 2). Generally, it is not possible to transfer probation orders to or from Northern Ireland, the Isle of Man or the Channel Islands, but an informal supervision can be done instead. The requirements to attend the probation centers, inapplicable in Scotland, should be taken in Northern Ireland as referring to "day centers" in the meaning of *The Probation Act (Northern Ireland) 1950* (s. 2B). Similarly, probation orders cannot be transferred to or from the Republic of Ireland, but supervision in probation and after-care cases may sometimes be possible on a voluntary basis.[28]

9.3. BREACH, REVOCATION AND DISCHARGE

9.3.1. BREACH. Procedure on breach is used, often not quite accurately, to describe two different circumstances: a failure to comply with a requirement of the order or the commission of a further offense during the probation period.

If a probationer fails to comply with one or more of the requirements of a probation order made by a magistrates' court, he is liable to be brought before the supervising court or before the court which made the order. The magistrates' court can either decide to continue or terminate the order. If it decides to continue the order, it may either fine the offender up to a maximum of £1,000, impose a maximum 60-hour community service order, or impose an attendance order, if the probationer is under 21; *CJA 1991*, Sch. 2, par. 3(1)(a-d). If the original probation order was made by the Crown Court, the offender must be sent back to the Crown Court, if the supervising court decided not to deal with the matter in one of the three ways which allows the order to continue. The Crown Court has an almost similar position as the supervising court. It may either impose a maximum £1,000 fine, or make a community service order, and in either case it may allow the probation order to continue; or it may terminate the order and sentence the offender for the original offense as if he had just been convicted of that offense before the Crown Court. The options for the probation order include a community service order, a fine, with no specified limit, and an attendance center order, if the offender is under 21. Alternatively, it may pass a custodial sentence or make a fresh probation order.

If the probationer was convicted of an offense committed during the probation period, he may be sentenced for the original offense, in which case the probation order would cease its effects.[29] But the court is not obliged to sentence the offender for the original offense; it may simply allow the probation order to continue for the original period, if it deems as necessary; *PCCA 1973*, s. 5(2), s. 8(1)(7). In case of two or more concurrent orders, the probationer is liable for each original offense.[30] If the order was made by a magistrates' court, then both the supervising court or another magistrates' court, with the supervising court's consent, can deal with the order if the conviction is before the magistrates' court. If the latter conviction is before the Crown Court, but the order was made by a magistrates' court, the Crown Court may deal with the original offense, but is limited to sentences which may be passed by a magistrates' court. If the probation order was made by the Crown Court, only the Crown Court can deal with it. The court may either allow the probation order to continue or pass any kind of sentence as it would have had there been no probation order, including a custodial sentence; *PCCA 1973*, s. 8 (6-9). Whatever sentence is passed, the original probation order comes to an end, although the court is not restricted to making a fresh probation order for an extra period of a maximum of 3 years.

The pre-1991 period did not excel in too consistent principles, either within or between probation areas, for determining the appropriate point in initiating the breach proceedings. Managers used to manipulate to some extent their "performance indicators" by tolerating absenteeism and sometimes by avoiding to trigger the breach proceedings.[31] *The CJA 1991* and the *National Standards 1992* stipulated a more rigorous set of rules in order to make the current practice more standardized and effective. The frequency of contacts was increased and the number of absences leading to breach was limited. In time, the results fell below expectations. The new regulations created a tense climate between probationers, supervisors, managers and courts, and resulted in a higher rate of breached orders. Critics talked about the tendency to impose on to the probation officers, whose rehabilitation philosophy was essentially optimistic, the "culture of severity" and the "pessimism" of the courts, both biased to develop a bleak view of the human nature, where failure becomes expected and success is disregarded.[32] Should courts use more flexible borderlines between the minimal requirements, namely the enforcement standards, and a good practice, that is, the availability for help, this danger would be avoidable.

In Scotland, breach of probation requirements and breach by further offense were set out by *The CPA (Scotland) 1975*, ss. 186-187, 387-388. The court has to recall the offender and either fine him for breaching the order, or have the order varied or terminated, in the latter case the offender being sentenced for the original offense. In Scotland, the court which holds the order has all the powers and responsibilities to deal with the breaches of that order, whether they be breaches of requirement or breaches by further offense, unlike the system in England and Wales, which makes a much greater play of distinctions between the different court levels and between different areas. The execution of a probation order made in Scotland for a resident or resident-to-be of England or Wales shall be supervised by a magistrates' court in that area of residence, irrespective of the level of the court which issued the order in Scotland. The execution of probation orders made in England and Wales for residents or residents-to-be of Scotland shall be supervised by the sheriff court of that area of residence, acting in its summary capacity. That means that the court in Scotland cannot deal with the original offense or a breach of requirement related to the original offense, but instead, it can send the probationer back to the original English or Welsh court.

9.3.2. REVOCATION AND DISCHARGE. By statute, both probation officer and offender can apply to the court to have the order revoked. Revocation is exercised by the supervising court, except when the Crown Court makes a probation order and specifically includes a direction reserving to itself the power of revoking the order; *CJA 1991*, Sch. 2, pars. 7-9. The order may be revoked for the probationer's *good progress* or if *supervision* proved to be *impracticable*. If the probationer applies, the supervising officer needs not to be summoned, but the court will normally require a report from him before it passes its decision.[33]

Revocations for good progress were recently scrutinized from an anti-discriminatory perspective. Before the *National Standards 1992*, early discharge was frequently used as a convenient way for both probation officers, for unloading the backlog of orders, and probationers, for lowering the risk of breaching. Practicing revocation as a routine was attractive for managers, who contributed to some extent to the "success" rates. On the other hand, the courts themselves were not always uncritical about this "practice", not to mention their low capacity to effectively monitor it; the applications gave insufficient information, and therefore, the court decisions were frequently taken in the absence of the parties. *The CJA 1991* and the *National Standards* have minimized the risk of resentencing for reoffending, giving the early discharge a superfluous advantage. Yet this traditional practice still has strong support among practitioners, managers, magistrates and even the Home Office. However, the consensus becomes less unanimous when they deal with the differentiation, somewhat anomalistic, between probation orders, which can be terminated for good progress, and community service orders, which cannot. Some even suggested that early termination should only be applied for exceptional circumstances.[34]

If the order is deemed as no longer appropriate, the court, instead of revoking it, may impose a conditional discharge for the original offense, for the same period as the original order. The probationer is discharged under the condition that he commits no further offense between the making of the order of conditional discharge and the expiration of the probation period; *PCCA 1973*, s. 11(1). The probationer is then treated as if the original order was one of conditional discharge.

Currently, the legislation employs a non-uniform terminology for the termination of a probation order, namely *discharge* (*PCCA 1973*, s. 11, still in force) and *revocation* (*CJA 1991*, Sch. 2), generating ambiguity in the legal interpretation and the court practice.[35] *The PCCA 1973* terminology should therefore be amended, not only to avoid confusion, but also to get a more flexible procedure for the 1973 Act, in accordance with the current regulations.

In Scotland, the possibilities for discharge are apparently underused.[36] The order can be discharged before the due date, if the probationer made a "good progress," which means a successful completion of the order. There is no legal bar to earlier applications but the first half of the probation period is usually considered as the minimum term before applying. Occasionally, discharge is necessary for administrative purposes. For instance, the court, imposing the custodial sentence for an offense committed during the probation period, cannot deal with the original offense; or it is competent to deal with it, but neglects to do so through administrative oversight; or, making a new probation order for the further offense, it neglects to deal with the original offense. For discharging the order, both the probation officer and, more rarely, the probationer may apply to the court; *CPA Scotland 1975*, Sch. 5, par. 1. A Scottish court supervising an order made in England or Wales can discharge that order, either on grounds of good progress, or when the probationer was sentenced with imprisonment for committing a new offense.

In the United States, revocation of probation is a result of breaching the order and can lead to the imposition of a custodial sentence. Revocation of probation is not viewed as part of the sentencing process,[37] but the probationer is entitled to the standard procedural guarantees, including a *hearing* with *notice* and the opportunity to be heard. Yet he is not entitled to appoint a counsel at the state expense unless the issues are complex or fundamental fairness requires otherwise.[38] However, the probation officers do not use uniform standards in revoking the orders. An older North Carolina study[39] reported, for instance, that the probation officer's residence could significantly alter the revoking patterns. To that extent, there are substantial differences between the *urban liberals* and the *rural conservatives*. The former tend to exceed all combinations of "unofficial" actions against "revocation" in instances involving the revoking pattern, extenuating circumstances, and points of exposure to official agencies or processes. The latter usually go less for an "unofficial" action. The rural conservatives have a predominant "social order" philosophy, and the reasons for their decisions to revoke are more "officer-oriented," in contrast with the urban liberals, who are "probationer-oriented."

In the late 1980s, the probation officer was given extended prerogatives in the revocation process, as a hearing officer in the preliminary hearing stage.[40] This role, outlined in the early 1970s by two Supreme Court cases,[41] can be viewed as a substantial change for the service. It diverted from the traditional functions of supervision and pre-sentence investigations of guilty clients, and required the officer to operate in a context in which there is a presumption of innocence rather than of guilt. According to the rules in force,[42] a probation officer, who must not have supervised the probationer at any time, is designated to conduct the preliminary interview; this is followed by a brief outlining of the hearing steps and a determination of the probable cause of the breach, a brief of the probationer's adjustment under supervision, and the available resources if a new supervision becomes necessary. The system brought certain economic advantages by lowering state financial costs, otherwise payable for the appointed counsel, a longer record and a possible judicial review.

There is already a substantial body of precedents supporting the authority of the American courts to revoke probation for inappropriate behavior *before* the commencement of the probation period, both for criminal and non-criminal conduct. Theoretical debates,[43] fueled by a heterogeneous practice,[44] questioned the court's authority to revoke probation for technical and non-criminal violations while the defendant was serving *split sentences*,[45] and argued the interference with the executive branch authority (the Parole Commission). Eventually, statutory provisions[46] granted the courts the right to revoke probation if the probationer breached a condition of the order before its termination. In the past, the court decisions grounded the revocation rationale on the principle of the "probation as a favor" granted for reformation. Accordingly, a violation, even non-criminal, would indicate less of a rehabilitation capacity than the court originally expected.[47] Furthermore, the decision to revoke probation has basically been a judicial function, preeminent in regard to executive authority. However, these violations must be reasonably serious and directly related to the offender's potential to successfully serve on probation.

9.3.3. FAILURE AND SUCCESS RATES. An early and constant interest in assessing probation effectiveness as to its failure and success rates has been shown by a series of research undertaken in the past 50 years, done mostly in the United States and Canada. Probation outcome was measured as a success or failure during supervision or the post-probation period. The definitions of failure, the follow-up periods, and the types of offenders employed in the samples varied from study to study and prevented an adequate assessment of probation or a determination of its effectiveness.[48] Failure was usually measured through reconviction (breach by further offense), revocation or absconding rates, although in many cases the definitions of a "failure" were not following uniform criteria. For instance, some studies used "failure" to indicate the "termination of the order due to reconviction, revocation, or absconding," while others deemed as "absconding" or "disappearance without notification" as not being "failures." Success was measured by the degree of completing the probation term without reconviction, revocation, or absconding. None of the analyzed studies have indicated the use of a control group for comparison, a very important factor in correctional research.[49] In order to assess post-probation outcome, different follow-up periods were used, ranging from 6 months to 11 years. Also, the subjects were selected on different criteria; while some studies used either felons only or both felons and misdemeanants, others did federal probationers or state probationers. In spite of its extensive use, probation has been the center of much controversy and criticism for its failure to satisfactorily rehabilitate and deter offenders placed under supervision. Partly, this was due to the decline of the rehabilitative ideal and the rise of the "just deserts" or the *justice model*. All in all, the analyzed research indicated that probation is relatively effective as a correctional alternative, the failure rates ranging from 14%[50] to 60%.[51] We have grouped the top 10 factors associated with failure and success in 3 types of variables, namely the *psycho-physical* (gender, age, race, behavior), the *socio-economic* (marital status, profession, education) and the *judicial variables* (criminal record, type of offense, degree of supervision). Young males, with a past history of disciplinary problems, unmarried, with a low socio-economic status and criminal record are more likely to fail. High failure rate is also linked with racial origin, the petty property offenses and intensive supervision.[52] Older probationers, married with children, highly trained, adequately employed, non-addicted (or receiving additional treatment), receiving a minimal supervision, and residing in the same area for more than 2 years, are more likely to be successful under the probation supervision. Lower failure rates were also reported for females, first offenders, violent, sex and drug offenders, and probationers given straight probation time (as opposed to the offenders given probation and jail time, and those given straight jail time).[53] Some associations can be outlined between the different polar variables, for instance: age - type of offense (young property offenders > adult violent and sex offenders), socio-economic status - type of offense (low income > property offenses), education - employment (low educational achievement > professional instability), behavior - criminal record (personal instability > prior convictions); see **Table 3**.

9.4. AMENDMENT

A probation order may be amended by the court with jurisdiction in the area where the probationer resides, called the *supervising court*. Both the probation officer and the probationer may apply for amendment. The supervising court may amend the order by either canceling any of its requirements, adding further requirements, or substituting one for another; *PCCA 1973*, Sch. 1, par. 3(1), as amended by *CJA 1991*, Sch. 2.

The amendment requires the offender's consent, unless it cancels or reduces the duration or a requirement and substitutes a new petty sessions area or a new place. The court can amend an order when the offender changes his residence.

A court shall not make amendments in order to include conditions related to psychiatric treatment or treatment against dependency on drugs or alcohol later than the first 3 months after the order was issued. The medical practitioner or other responsible person specified in the additional requirements for such categories of treatments is entitled to ask the probation officer in charge with the offender's supervision to apply for a variation or cancellation of the requirement in court.[54]

9.5. REHABILITATION

In certain cases, if an offender is not reconvicted within a stated period, called *rehabilitation period*, his convictions are deemed spent and are ignored. Once a conviction has become spent, the convicted person does not have to reveal it or admit its existence in most circumstances (e.g., when filling a form, or at an interview, for a job).

According to *The Rehabilitation of Offenders Act 1974* (in force since July 1, 1975), applicable in England, Wales and Scotland, the period depends on the gravity of the offense and the convictions resulting in custody for life or more than 2 and a half years are never "spent."[55] Initially, *The ROA 1974* fixed the rehabilitation term for probation orders and supervision orders to 1 year or to a period equal with the duration of the order, whichever is the longer; *ROA 1974*, s. 5, Table A. The supervision orders are applicable in England and Wales for offenders aged 10 to 17 years old; *The Children and*

Table 3: *Factors influencing the probation outcome*

VARIABLES		PROBATION FAILURE	PROBATION SUCCESS
PSYCHO	GENDER	males; (California B.S., 1977; Cuniff, 1986;	females (Davis, 1964; Frease, 1964; Wisconsin C.D., 1972; California B.S., 1977)
PHYSI-CAL	AGE	later-born probationer; (Mullin, 1973) younger offenders; (McCarthy & Langworthy, 1987) males in their mid-20s; (Cuniff, 1986) younger offenders under 30; (California B.S., 1977) youthfulness; (Caldwell, 1951; England, 1955;Missouri D.P.P., 1976; Bartell & Thomas, 1977; Roundtree, Edwards & Parker, 1984)	first-born probationer; (Mullin, 1973) older offenders; (McCarthy & Langworthy, 1987) older people over 28; (Bartell & Thomas, 1977) age 55 or older; (Kusuda, 1976) older people; (Davis, 1964)
VARIA-BLES	RACE	racial origin; (Cockerill,1975)	race; (Tippman, 1976; California B.S., 1977)
	BEHA-VIOR	personal instability; (England, 1955) antisocial behavior, past history of disciplinary problems; (Landis, Mercer & Wolff, 1969) alcohol and drug abuse; (Wisconsin C.D., 1972; Missouri D.P.P., 1976, Renner, 1978) marital status; (Cockerill, 1975)	non-drinking; (Frease, 1964) no drug abuse; (McCarthy & Langworthy, 1987) non-use of drugs and alcohol; (Kusuda, 1976) marital status; (Missouri D.P.P. 1976)
SOCIO-	MARITAL STATUS	marital status and number of dependents; (Kane County Diagnostic Center, no date) living at home with family; (Cuniff, 1986) unmarried; (Morgan, 1991) marital instability; (Landis, Mercer & Wolff, 1969)	positive family support; (Frease, 1964) married; (Frease, 1964; McCarthy & Langworthy, 1987) stable marriage; (Kusuda, 1976) marriage with children; (Caldwell, 1951) living with the spouse and/or child; (Petersilia, 1987)
ECONO MIC	PROFES-SIONAL STATUS	lower socio-economic status; (Landis, Mercer & Wolff, 1969) lower socio-economic background; (England, 1955) unemployment; Wisconsin C.D., 1972; Renner, 1978;New Jersey A.O.C., 1980; Scott & Carey, 1983; Morgan, 1991) professional instability; (Landis, Mercer & Wolff, 1969) problems related to employment; (Cockerill, 1975) low income/wage; (Petersilia, 1987; Morgan, 1991)	high occupational skills; (Caldwell, 1951) full-time employment; (Caldwell, 1951; Kusuda, 1976 McGinnis & Klockseim, 1976; Missouri D.P.P., 1976; McCarthy & Langworthy, 1987) stable income; (Kane County Diagnostic Center, no date; Kusuda, 1976; Petersilia, 1987) adequate income; (Caldwell, 1951; Missouri D.P.P., 1976)

Table 3 *continued*

VARI-ABLES		
EDUCA-TIONAL STATUS	lower grade of education; (Roundtree, Edwards & Parker, 1984) lower educational achievement; (Landis, Mercer & Wolff, 1969)	higher grade of education; (Frease, 1964) higher educational training/attainment; Kane County Diagnostic Center, no date; Missouri D.P.P., 1976)
CRIMINAL RECORD	previous criminal record; (England, 1955; New Jersey A.O.C., 1980; Roundtree, Edwards & Parker, 1984) juvenile/adult criminal record; (Landis, Mercer & Wolff 1969; Tippman, 1976) prior convictions; (Cockerill, 1975; California B.S., 1977; Petersilia, 1987; Morgan, 1991) prior incarceration; Kane County Diagnostic Center, no date; Missouri D.P.P., 1976; Scott & Carey, 1983)	no prior felony commitments; (Frease, 1964)
JUDI-CIAL		
TYPE OF OFFENSE	minor offenses; (Caldwell, 1951; Kusuda, 1976) minor offenses: gambling, theft, disorderly conduct; (England, 1955) minor offenses: forgery, check offenses; (Davis, 1964) property offenses; (Landis, Mercer & Wolff, 1969; California B.S., 1977; McCarthy & Langworthy, 1987; Petersilia, 1987; Morgan, 1991) property offenses: burglary; (Bartell & Thomas, 1977; Cuniff, 1986) forcible rape and property offenses: armed robbery, motor vehicle theft, forgery; (Missouri D.P.P., 1976) nonviolent offenders; (Holland, Holt & Beckett, 1982)	violent and drug offenses; (Petersilia, 1987) homicide and sex offenses; (Davis, 1964) sex offenders; (California B.S., 1977) usually violent offenders; (McCarthy & Langworthy, 1987)
VARI-ABLES		
DEGREE OF SUPER-VISION	long period of probation supervision; (Wisconsin C.D., 1972; Roundtree, Edwards & Parker, 1984) intensive supervision; (Lohman, 1966) longer and more intense periods of probation supervision; (Renner, 1978) probation and jail time offenders, straight jail time probationers; (California B.S., 1977)	minimal supervision; (Lohman, 1966) receiving additional alcohol treatment; (Ditman, 1967) straight offenders; (California B.S., 1977)

Author's table. Sources: J. B. Mullin, 1973; K. D. Morgan, 1993.

Young Persons Act 1969, as amended by *The CJA 1991*. The term has been subsequently extended to 5 years for probationers aged 18 or over, and to 2 and a half years or a period equal with the duration of the probation order, whichever is the longer, for the probationers under the age of 18 at the date of conviction; *The Criminal Justice and Public Order Act 1994*, Sch. 9, par. 11. The amendment reflected the change in status for probation, turned into a punishment by *The CJA 1991*.[56] It also brought the term into line with the one provided for community service orders and combination orders, but it created an inconsistency with the one provided for supervision orders, which remained 1 year or the duration of the order, whichever is the longer, according with *The CYPA 1969*.[57] Spent convictions will be kept in the official records, without being disclosed to others, unless there is an official reason for doing so. *The ROA 1974* reads that spent convictions may still be mentioned in criminal or juvenile cases, and in civil cases only if the court is satisfied that justice cannot be done without disclosing a spent conviction. Also, according to the 1974 Act, employers cannot refuse to hire or to fire somebody merely because the employee once had a spent conviction.

CHAPTER 10

CASELAW

10.1. UNITED KINGDOM

10.1.1. ELIGIBILITY. Before making a probation order the court shall explain to the offender in ordinary language the effect of the order and the consequences of failure to comply with it or of the commission of another offense.[1] A probation order must not be made unless the offender expresses his willingness to comply with the requirements of the order, having been given a fair opportunity to make the choice.[2] Consent must be genuine. The court held that consent was invalid and, accordingly, the probation order was void where an offender unwillingly consented to the making of a probation order on the understanding that the only other measure which could be considered was a custodial sentence, when on the facts of the offense this was "an exceedingly remote alternative."[3]

Where the offender receives a suspended sentence for an offense, the court which imposes the suspended sentence may not make a probation order in respect of another offense for which he is dealt with by the court; *PCCA 1973*, s. 22(3). The statutory prohibition against the making of a probation order at the same time as a suspended sentence is passed applies whether the two offenses concerned are charged in the same indictment[4] or different indictments.[5] This does not preclude the making of either a suspended sentence or a probation order when the other measure is already current. If a magistrates' court wished to make a probation order on a defendant subject to a Crown Court suspended prison sentence, the proper course would be to commit him to Crown Court so that the whole matter could be considered together.[6] It is not desirable for a suspended prison term and a probation order to run at the same time. Though if a defendant is already subject to a suspended sentence, it might be preferable to add a condition of supervision to that sentence.[7]

A probation order should not be made when the offender is sentenced at the same time to a custodial sentence in respect of another offense.[8] A subsequent custodial measure for another offense does not automatically terminate a probation order, which will thus continue, unless specifically dealt with by the court, and will resume on the probationer's release.[9] A probation order may not be made in respect to a person adjudged guilty of contempt of court.[10] On the other hand, where an offender is subject to two committals in respect of different offenses, and is dealt with in respect of one of them by means of a probation order by a sentencer who is aware of the other matter, it may be inappropriate for a sentencer dealing with the second matter to impose a custodial sentence.[11]

A probation order may not be made to commence on a day other than the day on which it is made.[12] Where the offender is subject to more than one probation order at the same time, each is effective in the case of a further conviction or breach of a requirement of the order for the purpose of sentencing him for the offense for which it was imposed but only the most recent is effective for the purpose of supervision.[13]

The CJA 1991 contains a range of statutory criteria governing the use of community sentences (s. 6). The court can impose such a sentence if it is satisfied that the offense or the concurrent offenses are *serious enough*. The choice of a particular community sentence must be based on *suitability* for the offender and the fact that the *restriction on liberty* imposed by the order must be commensurate with the *gravity* of the offense or the offenses associated with it. But an offense may not be regarded as more serious by reason of any previous convictions of the offender or any failure to respond to previous sentences (s. 29). In fact, the courts were flexible in this matter even before the 1991 Act; they held that a probation order may be appropriate even in the case of a persistent offender when there are factors which may indicate that "it is worth taking a risk to see if [his] lifelong pattern of offending can be broken."[14]

10.1.2. CONDITIONS. If the court simply says that it makes a probation order, the effect is an order requiring the probationer to be under the supervision of a probation officer for the period specified. If the court desires to impose other conditions, they must be specified. It was held that the use of a probation order in order to recover money which was not subject to charge was improper.[15]

Some alleged that the condition according to which the probationer "should lead an honest and industrious life" is extremely vague. Since the consequences for committing a further offense are provided by statute, this requirement should probably be taken as an abstention on behalf of the probationer to do something that could amount to a criminal offense, which, in practice, is difficult for the court to deal with.[16]

In addition, a probation order may require the offender to comply during the whole of, or any part of, the probation period with such requirements as the court, having regard to the circumstances of the case, considers necessary for securing the good conduct of the offender or for preventing a repetition by him of the same offense or the commission of other offenses, except payment of damages or compensation. But the power to impose such requirements must be subject to some limitation. For instance, the court must not introduce a custodial or other element that will amount in substance to the imposition of a sentence. Any discretion conferred on the probation officer must be confined within well-defined limits, since it is the court alone which can define the requirements of the order.[17]

As to the residence requirements, the court should first consider the offender's home surroundings.[18] Bailing a defendant to a probation hostel for assessment, instead of committing him to prison, in the hope that he might react favorably, has been considered a "valuable weapon in sentencing."[19]

The condition to undergo medical treatment has been employed to facilitate the administration of antiabuse tablets prescribed by the doctor but administered by the probation officer.[20] By statute, the probation officer responsible for the in-patient supervision should carry it out only to the extent it is deemed necessary for the purpose of discharging or amending the order; *PCCA 1973*, s. 3(4). Sometimes, this curtailment of responsibility is ignored "in the interests of good practice."[21] The doctor, with the probationer's consent, can arrange for treatment in a center not specified in the order, including in-patient treatment, which means the original order is amendable without being referred back to the court. Nonetheless, there could be a subsequent query as to the validness of a consent given in the respective circumstances. Refusal or a non-cooperative attitude with the treatment is usually a *prima facie* breach of probation.[22] But refusal to undergo a surgical, electrical or the like treatment, having regard to all the circumstances, may not be treated as a failure to comply with that requirement.

Where an offender is in danger of becoming seriously addicted to drugs, the sentencer may be qualified in making a probation order, if this course appears likely to be effective in countering the tendency toward addiction, even though his offense would otherwise justify a substantial term of imprisonment.[23]

10.1.3. BREACH, REVOCATION AND DISCHARGE. Where a probationer is sentenced for a breach of requirement or on conviction for a further offense, any order for compensation remains in force.[24]

There is no power to deal with a probationer where the conviction within the period of probation is for an offense committed *before* the probation order was made.[25] There is power to deal with him where the conviction is recorded after the period expires, if the offense was committed *during* the period of probation. If the conviction is quashed, there is no power to deal with him for a breach of probation.[26]

When the probationer commits an offense while on probation, the court should consider whether he is to be dealt with for the original offense, otherwise it cannot be counted subsequently as a conviction (e.g., for purposes of qualifying for an extended prison sentence). The probation officer's responsibility stands until the order is discharged, even if the probationer is in custody.[27] A subsequent conviction to probation has to deal with the initial breach of order.[28] The probationer who committed a further offense during the probation term will be sentenced for the original offense. If the court concurrently deals with the original offense and the further offense, it should separately adjudicate the original offense. The sentence for the original offense should make the probationer understand that probation discharge is not a mere formality.[29]

If the probationer is subsequently convicted by the Crown Court, this court also has jurisdiction for the original offense,[30] since it sits as a single indivisible court.[31]

The court has full discretion in using its prerogatives. In dealing with the original offense, it shall consider the existing circumstances both before and after the probation order.[32] The court may either: impose a punitive sentence, such as a fine or custody, which will terminate the initial probation order; impose a new probation order or other individualized measure; ignore the offense and allow the initial order to continue unaffected. Many courts deem as incorrect the philosophy of regarding the new offense as more serious *per se* and, therefore, deserving custody simply because it repeated a previous offense treated leniently at the time; all cases must be viewed in the light of their particular facts and the offender must be given "a final chance" where appropriate.[33]

Crown Court, in turn, may either impose a fine or a community service order, provided there are appropriate conditions for such an order, or deal with the probationer for the offense as if he had just been convicted before the Crown Court of that offense,[34] including the power to make a fresh probation order. The latter option is practiced in exceptional circumstances only.[35] A possible effect of making a second probation order for the original offense is a supervision period exceeding 3 years.[36]

If a probation order is made on appeal, it is regarded as made by the court who convicted the offender, for the purposes of enforcement.[37] If the probationer breached an order made by the Court of Appeal, the sentencing court should regard that he already served either the whole or part of his sentence before the order was made and should deal with the original offense accordingly; otherwise, he would be punished twice for the same offense.[38]

The Court of Appeal has frequently stressed the importance of observing the strict procedural standards applicable to probationers. The court should be satisfied that the probationer was previously informed about his original conviction and probation order, and the consequences he would face in case of breaching the order or committing a new offense. Then he should be asked if he admits the original offense and the making of the order, and if he does, the courts should proceed. If he does not admit those matters, then the making of the order must be strictly proved by a person who was in court when the probation order was made. The subsequent conviction must also be formally proven.[39]

The essential feature of probation is supervision; where the offender does not require or is unlikely to respond to such supervision, or where supervision will be impractical because of the offender's occupation, the court will impose a different sanction.[40] A deportation order will not discharge the original probation order.[41]

10.1.4. AMENDMENT. The supervising probation officer has the duty to seek amendment of an order whenever he considers necessary. The amendment appears necessary when the probationer is moving to a new petty sessions area, unless the officer believes he will not reside there long enough, or ascertains that the court of the new area was satisfied that special circumstances imposed maintaining the same supervision officer in charge.[42]

The order remains the official responsibility of the existing supervisor in the original area until the order is amended to include the new petty sessions area. In the meantime, a probation officer from the new area may exercise *de facto* the supervision.

10.2. UNITED STATES OF AMERICA

10.2.1. ELIGIBILITY. Basically, probation is designed to promote rehabilitation.[43] The probationer need never serve a day in prison. The conditions imposed on his liberty and the guidance afforded by a trained officer provide the necessary control, direction, and encouragement for this rehabilitation process. Because of the limited funds and supervisory staff, it is particularly important to place on probation only those offenders with potential for reform. Many courts use pre-sentence investigation reports as aids in determining who should be granted probation, though the process of determining the factors assessing individual potential for rehabilitation through conditional liberty remains a difficult task. As a result, the use of probation in different jurisdictions varies considerably.[44] The most common factors used in selection are age, prior record, current offense and psychological stability.[45] The offense is regarded as a critical factor in the selection process. Offenders with strong family ties, stable jobs, and higher education are likely to have better rehabilitation records when placed on probation than those lacking such attributes.[46]

10.2.2. CONDITIONS. The statutes following *The Probation Act 1878* were consistently silent as to the conditions required for probation. *The Federal Probation Act 1925* authorized the courts to make probation orders for such period and upon such terms and conditions as they may deem best, if they were satisfied that the ends of justice and the best interest of the public, as well as the defendant will be subserved.[47] Nearly all state statutes followed a similar pattern. Only a few states attempted to list conditions in their statutes.[48] The lack of guidelines led some courts to impose requirements seriously affecting the probationer's freedom.[49] By the same token, they overturned the revocation of the order, if based on vague conditions.[50] On the contrary, other courts upheld the revocation based on implied conditions or statutory requirements, despite the fact that the probationer was not explicitly informed of them.[51] Therefore, the probationer should receive adequate notice of what is demanded of him.[52] An implied condition, such as "not to break the law," should only extend to illegal conduct which displays a failure to accept rehabilitative treatment and poses a definite risk to society, or to the commission of felonies.[53] In any case, probation revocation based on such an implied condition should only occur after a proper adjudication of guilt for the new offense.[54] Conditions should be reasonably related to the purposes of the probation statutes[55] and not be dependent on events beyond the probationer's control. They should not be exceedingly harsh to unnecessarily encourage breaches or turn a basically positive reform program into a negative coercion.[56] Probation term should be a fixed term and should not be altered without cause, although some state statutes allowed courts to extend the term[57] and alter the original conditions.[58] Those amendments should not be done merely on the suggestion of the supervising officer,[59] but after a thorough investigation of the reasons for change.

Initially, courts used to have a large discretion when dealing with conditions that might offer a more effective rehabilitation. Probation itself was regarded as merely a legislative grace, that is a favor not a right. In an older decision, the Supreme Court stated that a probationer had no constitutional right to be granted or to retain his probation,[60] an opinion which allowed the state legislatures to vest the courts with discretionary powers in the matter.[61] Other states distanced themselves from this traditional view, by providing in their constitutions certain rights for probationers, such as some procedural guarantees during the revocation proceedings.[62]

Some jurisdictions required the defendant to accept probation when "granted"[63] based on the rationale that probation was not a "punishment" in the meaning of the federal Constitution, since its purpose is not a punitive one. Yet the defendant's consent should not be taken as a waiver of the Eighth Amendment, which prohibits the infliction of cruel and unusual punishments, when faced with the coercive alternative of a long prison term. Accordingly, the defendant may oppose that condition as unconstitutional, if he deems it as extremely harsh and having little rehabilitative value, and may choose between other forms of punishment.

The condition requiring the probationer to refrain from committing further offenses during the term of probation can be valid on its face, but can also lead to constitutionally questionable results. Due to the low standard of proof required in a revocation proceeding, a probationer could, for instance, be sent to prison, although he might be found innocent for committing the new offense in a subsequent trial.[64]

The condition requiring the offender to make restitution to the victim or cover the damages, in the absence of any claim or court order, should be regarded as violating the right of due process.[65]

These shortcomings are avoidable or minimized by granting the probationer a larger set of procedural guarantees.

10.2.3. REVOCATION. As mentioned before, courts regarded probation as a device with no constitutional protection. Due process clause would be inapplicable,[66] because probation was viewed as a privilege or a legislative grace;[67] by accepting probation, the defendant would enter into a contract with the state, waiving his due process rights.[68] Other courts argued that probation would not substantially differ from imprisonment since the probationer was however "within the constructive custody of the court;"[69] therefore, revocation was not a "criminal prosecution"[70] giving the probationer the constitutional rights he used to have and exhausted in the trial stage.[71] Reluctance to apply constitutional standards to probation in general and to its revocation in particular was supported by the very limited nature of the probationer's statutory rights. The Supreme Court outlined this restrictive right v. privilege-based distinction philosophy in *Escoe v. Zerbst* (1935).[72]

Few state statutes explicitly enumerated which procedural guarantees were to be afforded and which were not.[73] Some states expressly authorized revocation with no hearing,[74] while others, like California,[75] were not specific on this matter.[76] As a result, some courts held there was no right to hearing when the order was revoked.[77] Yet the majority of state statutes, by using different wording,[78] required a hearing of some sort,[79] even summary in nature.[80] Some courts interpreted the limited character of probation statutory rights as an interdiction to afford further rights.[81] Failure to exercise certain procedural rights at the revocation hearing was taken as a waiver.[82] Frequently, the statutes do not grant for a probationer the right to subpoena witnesses or to obtain appointment of counsel, if indigent.[83] The standard of proof which governs the revocation hearing is usually low. The order can be simply revoked if evidence "reasonably satisfies" the court,[84] such as a probation officer's report, even erroneously made, on the alleged improper activity done by a probationer.[85]

If the probationer cannot appeal against revocation, he must seek a writ of *habeas corpus*, and certain procedural irregularities revisable on appeal cannot be raised at the next proceeding.[86] If appeal is permitted, the state is required to produce only "some" evidence to support revocation,[87] while the probationer, in order to obtain a reversal, has to prove the court abused its wide discretion,[88] an evidence rarely proven in the appellate court.[89] The early probation statutes appeared to have followed the court's loose discretionary approach.[90]

However, the trend is toward a larger procedural protection of probationers.[91] Many state courts have already recognized the probationer's right to a hearing and to a notice of the charges against him,[92] retained counsel,[93] the presentation of evidence,[94] the cross-examination of adverse witnesses,[95] and the appeal.[96] In the last decades, the *right v. privilege* theory has been seriously questioned, and some argued that, for reasons of accuracy and policy, the terms "privilege," "grace" and "favor" should only apply to the court's discretion to grant probation, not to the continuance of the probationer's conditional liberty.[97] It is true that the probationer has no more constitutional rights than the prisoner at the moment of sentencing; but having been granted a liberty which the prisoner does not have, the probationer is in a position to claim certain constitutional rights which the prisoner cannot. Courts, taking over this viewpoint, held that substantive rights would be of little value without procedural methods which would enable their presentation,[98] and that there was no absolute distinction between "rights" and "privileges" but simply a different degree of protection. A probation order can be revoked only if breached, and not in an arbitrarily manner.[99] They have extended the procedural rights both to pre-trial[100] and post-conviction[101] stages.

Development of probation programs have also influenced the court policy in revocation proceedings. For instance, courts revoked the order in the case where a probationer failed to make victim restitution,[102] since restitution was not merely viewed as a repay but a way of punish and reform. By the same token, it was held that psychological counseling was compulsory, unless it forced the probationer to undergo drug therapy or to be placed in seclusion.[103]

From the perspective that many probationer's procedural rights have already been statutorily provided, their eventual constitutional consecration would not apparently overburden the U.S. probation system. On the contrary, this will result in a better adjustment between probation facts and goals. Nowadays, it is largely the staff experience that makes probation work efficiently. Therefore, a series of improvements on the constitutional level would eliminate much of the error, uncertainty, confusion and geographic inequity which presently prevail.

CONCLUSIONS

Probation has its origins in two distinct traditions, the common law and the civil (statute) law, largely convergent after World War II. While the civil law countries softened their formalism given the Anglo-Saxon influence, the common law countries started to codify probation, formerly a creation of courts.

But probation has developed differently within the common law system itself. In the United Kingdom, emergence of probation was largely a reflection of dissatisfaction with the nineteenth century penological theories about the "uniform treatment," whose damaging consequences in prisons were in obvious contrast with the optimism inspired by police court missionaries. Continental European positivism, Christian reformism and British administrative pragmatism made differentiation and individualism take over uniformity as a governing principle of national penal policy. A shift to probation reflected the belief that influence upon the offender would be better exercised if based on wise advice, good example, care and control, elements to be found in a respectable family which many offenders had been deprived of. Probation ideology remains libertarian, offender-oriented and anti-oppressive, while the job itself has become more control-oriented.

In the United States, the earliest probation assumed the same features of a humanitarian mission. In time, it rendered consonant with a cultural model in which caring for criminals was less acceptable than in those European countries where social explanations of crime prevailed. The importance of the Constitution and the relative autonomy of the communities, so far as operational probation was concerned, created a heterogeneous caselaw, and triggered conflicts between Supreme Court interpretations of the Constitution and the common law tradition. Historically, these conflicts referred to the court's power to suspend the constitutional rights of a defendant, when placed on probation (e.g., to make an order before a final sentence), or while in probation (e.g., to revoke an order only in a court hearing). In spite of a caseload comprising some 25% serious offenders, the American version of probation has kept its correctional orientation geared to law enforcement. On the other hand, its decentralized nature, given the large range of units nationwide, has created considerable resource pressures in some jurisdictions and a lack of effective monitoring standards.

In other former British colonies, probation followed a similar process of distancing itself from its common law origin. Canada, Australia, New Zealand and India imported probation from the metropolis, but import was quickly overlaid by local features. Cultural norms and geographic distance, together with material (available resources), political (reluctance toward overtolerance to offenders) and administrative factors (sophistication and responsiveness of the local authority structure) have all influenced development of probation. In the Canada and Australia due to the absence of a political will and the administrative capacity to generate a coherent system, probation was slow to develop. The vast and sparsely populated terrains made supervision an impractical measure, not to mention the evident lack of enthusiasm for offender-care, reasons for which probation attracted little attention before World War II. But even after, while Europe embraced a practice based on positivist criminology, where therapeutic function was deemed as a necessary corrective to legalism, Canada, Australia and New Zealand regarded probation as less a caring or therapeutic agency than as an instrument of community punishment. As to India, probation failed to develop into a responsive system, due to both geographic factors, widespread poverty and internal strife in a fragile democracy, which ensured that probation would remain a low political priority.

By the same token, the civil law countries adopted the common law device of probation in a differentiated manner, reflected in the distinct roles played in supervision by the voluntary organizations, the Church and members of the community. For instance, in Protestant countries like Germany, the Netherlands, and the Scandinavian states, the civil law tradition was tenuous, while links with England and the United States were stronger, as opposed to the other Western European countries, mostly Catholic, which followed closer the Franco-Belgian *sursis* model.

As to the Eastern European states, they followed the Franco-Belgian model in their pre-Communist period; during communism, probation was based on a collectivist system supervision performed by families and youth organizations for minor offenders, and workmates and trade unions for adult offenders. The system was abolished in post-Communism and the construction of new supervision systems is currently in progress. Political changes imposed new visions on the philosophy of probation. Eastern European countries, although a formerly unitary bloc, are extremely diverse and differentiated in culture, religion, and civilization. In considering whether Eastern European states should adopt one or more Western models of probation, it is worth mentioning that probation cannot be decoupled from the time and place in which it operates, or from the political, cultural and historical baggage it brings with it. In order to successfully solve the local problems of criminal justice and diversify the range of sentencing options available to courts, probation should first reflect local cultural norms and the political goals of the moment.

PART THREE

IMPLEMENTING MODELS

CHAPTER 11

LEGAL REFORM
IN TRANSITIONAL SOCIETIES

Finding suitable alternative models and implementing them efficiently stand as top priority issues not only for the Western criminal legislators' agenda. In the Eastern part of Europe there has been and still is active preoccupation for finding feasible solutions in order to flexibly remodel national criminal policies. Yet the facts of the past eight years prove that finding the best solution is not an easy task to perform.

In an early stage of the post-Cold War era, Western legal system standards were subject to study, reflection and debate on both individual, community and national levels. Then, the post-Communist lawmakers hastened the import of Western advanced legal devices as a magical solution to quickly end the disastrous effects of the collectivist ideology on economy and society. The paradox was that the modern and viable concepts of a developed society applied on an infrastructure of poverty, misery, anarchy, and corruption generated social dysfunction. Borrowing humanitarian laws, suitable for wealthy and stable societies, proved to be inefficient in the presence of poverty, social and political instability.[1] The rapid depreciation of life standards for the many and the rise of ostentatious prosperity for the new and few prosperous entrepreneurial elite minimized the public tolerance for a humane system of sanctions, reversing to a certain extent the initial post-Communist liberalization of criminal law.[2] Yet these factors were responsible for public intolerance only on the surface. Under the communist regimes, the execution of punishment was regarded both as a measure to combat crime and a as political weapon. For decades, the offender was regarded not only as an anti-social individual but as an enemy of the "working class" then in power, and his criminal impulses were deemed as "remnants of the old (i.e., capitalist) society." The former communist policies were to reshape his personality by inhuman treatment and harsh penalties, with stress on isolation from the outside world. In the 1970s, with the offensive of rehabilitative ideals, repression was softened, but not backed up with an adequate social care network. The result was a spectacular crime rate,[3] and the principles of retributive justice returned to favor.

The 1990s have recorded the same swinging evolution. The early 1990s were marked by national governments' constant efforts to adopt a more balanced criminal policy and to put their domestic legal systems in line with international standards.[4] First, this has been accomplished by extending the offender's rights and procedural guarantees and humanizing the execution of penalties. Secondly, victim rights were strengthened in the trial stage. The literature advanced ambivalent theories, such as the "dual humanism" in Russia,[5] or the "humanized retribution" in Poland,[6] which were reflecting the new legislative trends.

But in the mid-1990s, criminal activities intensified. Some people equated democracy with anarchy, and prosperity with vice. Then, transition to a free market economy was accompanied by massive unemployment rates, and more people became involved in criminal gangs to make a living. At the same time, Eastern Europe meant a new "market" for international organized crime, which turned countries like Bulgaria, Romania, Russia and Republic of Georgia into "transit states" for their illicit activities. All these factors increased public hostility towards any tendency of liberalism in criminal policy. In countries ruled at the time by reform communists, like Romania until 1996, the public suspected, not totally ungrounded, that the administration was using liberal international standards as a breach to spare some leaders from the communist past.[7]

Currently, the high crime rates again challenge East European lawmakers to enforce stiffer penalties and harsher conditions of confinement.[8] But the major premise underlying the Communist penal law, according to which effectiveness of crime control depends mostly on the intensity of punishment, should be turned down. A reasonable efficiency requires that humanism should not preclude a higher limit of punishment, where appropriate, but instead be combined with other objectives of criminal policy. Nowadays, things have reached a point where there is no prevailing theory of punishment, but various approaches often based on opposing theses, which coexist peacefully. Public opinion is similarly divided, swinging between the extremes of excessive harshness, by calling for more severe penalties and retention of the death penalty, and generous leniency, by moderating the idea of criminal liability. As a result, lawmakers seeking feasible Western models have created instead hybrid bodies of legislation, leaving an open door for the most diverse anti-crime strategies. Therefore, a mature criminal policy, far from extremes, should be a prerequisite for a comprehensive reform of the sentencing framework. An adequate selection of the Western statutory, strategic and technological products may offer options not for a more intensive but for a more varied system of penalties.

CHAPTER 12

OPTIONS FOR A PUNISHMENT REFORM

In order to achieve a more flexible and varied system of penalties, with a higher degree of fairness, equity and proportionality, expanding the range of alternatives becomes a necessity. The Western concerns are primarily related to the opportunity of a more varied system of alternatives,[1] or, at least, to the desirability to extend the range of models between probation and imprisonment.[2] On the contrary, post-Communist states, whose sanctioning framework was fitted for decades on the *fine-correctional labor-imprisonment* triplet, appears to be more responsive to the whole plethora of more or less traditional non-custodial alternatives. When fine has to sanction individual budgets in constant depreciation, and correctional labor is viewed as a burden for market-run company managers, the courts confront themselves with new sentencing strategies which should be promptly reflected by the statute law.

Under the circumstances, non-custodial alternatives appear to respond much better to a series of topical issues which post-Communist penal systems are currently confronted with. As mentioned already, in a time when no specific theory of punishment seems to prevail there is large room left to apply various strategies.

Alternative sanctions are, broadly speaking, better able than custody to encompass the main goals of punishment, that is *deterrence, incapacitation, rehabilitation* and *retribution*. Their diversity allows focus to be put on each of these objectives. The *mediation projects*, involving restitution payments and/or victim compensation, could be implemented as independent, or rather supplemental, conditions to other alternatives, especially for young offenders. *Day-fines*, with their particular retaliative nature, can be geared to the gravity of offense and the offender's financial availability, taking into account both the *just desert* principle and personal circumstances. Their flexible execution (payable in extendible installments) recommends them as a feasible option for the traditional fine. Classical community-based corrections, like *community service* and *probation*, have traditionally emphasized the offender's rehabilitation, by maintaining community and family ties. Supervising officers act as counselors whose primary duty is to help the offender to adjust himself to society. These alternatives proved to be efficient against short-term imprisonment, unless they are burdened by too many conditions. Their flexibility allows them to be coupled with a wide range of treatment programs, including residential care. They are cost-effective and their intensive use will lower the number of inmates and lead to big savings for prison administration. In spite of some important changes, community-based sanctions are likely to continue as the most popular alternatives used by Western courts. This is equally due to their flexibility and the presence of a high-trained specialized staff. The public's feeling of insecurity can be alleviated by implementing a whole new family of alternative sanctions, developed primarily to lower the stress created by classical surveillance and control. They are programs which, alongside traditional rehabilitative ideals, develop new dimensions of a more intensive control, turning themselves into genuine "alternatives to alternatives." These intermediate sanctions, being more punitive than probation, fall between traditional alternatives and custody. Control and surveillance are regarded as primary objectives, while rehabilitation becomes the secondary goal. They could be the ideal option for post-totalitarian societies, which are more conservative and usually less tolerant towards deviant behaviors, and still attractive for the rehabilitationists, as alternatives to custody. Such alternatives, including but not limited to, *intensive probation supervision, shock probation* and *split sentences, electronic monitoring, house arrest* and *residential community corrections*, and *shock incarceration* or the *boot camps*, combine intensive supervision with short-term custody or can be combined between themselves, offering "cocktail punishments" targeted to specific offender groups, such as property offenders or probation and parole violators. They can be administered by probation departments or jointly operated with correctional departments. Their effectiveness has not been confirmed in the majority of cases,[3] because of their multiple, restrictive and partly stigmatizing conditions,[4] but they are viewed as the "waiting room" for custody and a last rehabilitative resort for those categories of offenders. Estimates indicated that they were successful, delivered more services than would normally be received by probationers, and produced recidivism rates equal to or better than those of offenders who have been confined.[5] They fulfill multiple goals, such as *diversion* (non-custodial option), *control* (higher degree of security than probation), and *reintegration* (by maintaining community ties and being oriented toward a more productive lifestyle).[6]

Employed in this perspective, intermediate sanctions offer a viable solution for the critical problem of prison overcrowding, and are less costly than prison (though more expensive than probation).[7] Finally, they can build the successive steps of a non-custodial sanction "ladder," thereby restoring fairness and equity to non-incarceration sentences;[8] see **Table 4**.

Used frequently and diversely the whole set of non-custodial alternatives is the reflection of the triple imperative which every national criminal justice system is currently facing, that is *care - control - economy*, each of the terminals being connected with the three involved beneficiaries, namely *the offender - the public - the state*. The offender, assisted by specialized services, is concerned about the extent to which society is willing to offer him reintegration in the community; on the other hand, the public is concerned about the degree of security it is going to receive from the state; the state, in turn, is concerned about the costs of the criminal justice system as a whole. Alternative sanctions can satisfy all these needs, by offering: to the *offender*, a wide range of non-custodial programs, where treatment components prevail or play important roles; to the *public*, a diversity of crime control strategies; and to the *state*, cost-effective solutions without widening the net of the criminal justice system. With those trumps, backed up by an effective and efficient management, they are likely to grow and evolve in the following years, by significantly remodeling the sentencing system at the turn of the centuries.

Table 4: *The punishment scale*

FREEDOM RESTRICTION DEGREE (0-VI)	NONE (0)	MINIMUM (I)	MEDIUM LOW (II)	MEDIUM (III)	MEDIUM HIGH (IV)	HIGH (V)	TOP HIGH (VI)
RETRIBUTIVE INTENSITY LEVEL (0-30)		Limitations	Conditional liberty	Supervision	Supervision + custody	Custody	Death
0	-absolute discharge						
1	-admonition						
2	-conditional discharge						
3		-fine					
4		-day-fine					
5		-restitution					
6		-compensation					
7		-forfeiture/ confiscation					
8		-deprivation of certain rights					
9		-disqualification					
10			-suspended/ conditional sentence				
11				-probation			
12				-combination order (probation + community service)			
13				-intensive probation supervision			
14				-community service			
15				-correctional labor			
16					-electronic monitoring		
17					-curfew order		
18					-house arrest		
19					-weekend imprisonment		
20					-residential community center		
21					-attendance center		
22					-probation day center		
23					-day reporting center		
24					-split sentence		
25					-shock probation		
26						-shock incarceration (boot camp)	
27						-semi-open detention	
28						-fixed-term imprisonment	
29						-life detention	
30							-death penalty

Author's table.

NOTES

CHAPTER 1: AN OVERVIEW

1. *The First United Nations Congress on the Prevention of Crime and the Treatment of Offenders* adopted "The Standard Minimum Rules for the Treatment of Prisoners" (see UN Publication, Sales No. 56.IV.4, Annex I-A), a landmark in the process of penal reform. Later, the deliberations of the Fifth Congress brought to the fore the global search for effective alternatives to imprisonment, dealing with those offenders who do not endanger the peace and security of society (see *Fifth United Nations Congress on the Prevention of Crime and the Treatment of Offenders*, UN Publication, Sales No. E.76.IV.2. and Corr. 1, Chapter II, par. 268). The Sixth United Nations Congress on the Prevention of Crime and the Treatment of Offenders, held at Caracas (1980), debated the "Deinstitutionalization of corrections and its implications for the residual prisoner," while stressing the alternatives to imprisonment (UN Doc. A/CONF.87/7).

2. Between 1983-1992, the number of inmates increased with more than 20% in France, Greece, Ireland, the Netherlands, Portugal, Spain, Sweden and Switzerland. In Belgium, Denmark, Italy, England and Wales, the rate was modest (c.10%), while other countries recorded falls: Austria (-18%), Germany (-28%), Romania (-51.78%) and Finland (see Martin Killias et al., *The European Sourcebook of Crime and Criminal Justice Statistics (Draft Model)*, Strasbourg, European Committee on Crime Problems, 1995, pp. 124-125; Comisia Nationala de Statistica, *Anuarul Statistic al Romaniei 1993*, Bucharest, 1994, p. 645). The falls were the result of a series of measures such as limitation or abolition of short prison sentences (Germany, 1969; Austria, 1975), promotion of parole (Germany, 1986; Austria, 1988), large amnesty decrees (Romania, 1988), or other statutory measures (Finland) (A.

Kuhn, "Punitivite, politique criminelle et surpeuplement carceral," in: *Schweizerische Kriminologische Untersuchungen*, Bern, Verlag Paul Haupt, 1993; K. Sessar, "Substituts aux peines d'emprisonnement en Republique Federale d'Allemagne - principe et mise en oeuvre," in: *Revue de Science Penale et de Criminologie*, 1989, October-December; P. Tornudd, "Fifteen years of decreasing prisoner rates in Finland," Statement prepared for the hearing of the Western Australian Study Group's *Official Visit to Examine Policies and Strategies to Reduce the Rate of Imprisonment*, Vienna, 29 June 1991; Ulla V. Bondeson, "The Problems of Imprisonment," in: Roger Hood (ed.), *Crime and Criminal Policy in Europe: Proceedings of a European Colloquium*, Oxford, Center for Criminological Research, 1989, p. 223; Tiberiu Dianu, "The Evolution of Capital Punishment in Romania," in: *Revue Roumaine des Sciences Juridiques*, 1995, 2, pp. 185-186, 188.

3. Between 1982-1991, average detention increased considerably in Spain (from 4.8 to 7.3 months), the Netherlands (from 1.6 to 2.9 months); see also M. Killias, *supra 2*, p. 125.

4. United Nations, *Methods and ways likely to be most effective on preventing crime and improving the treatment of offenders*, Doc. E/CN.5/536, Annex IV, par. 47; United Nations, *Human rights in the administration of justice: note by the secretary-general*, Doc. E/AC.57/24 and Add. 1.

5. The National Swedish Council for Crime Prevention, *A New Penal System*, Report No. 5, Stockholm, 1978; E. Backman et al., *Finnish Criminal Policy in Transition*, Helsinki, University of Helsinki, Department of Criminal Law, 1979.

6. Douglas Lipton, Robert Martinson, Judith Wilks, *The Effectiveness of Correctional Treatment*, New York, Praeger, 1975; J. Wilson, *Thinking About Crime*, New York, Basic Books, 1975.

7. A. Dershowitz, *Fair and Certain Punishment*, New York, McGraw-Hill, 1976; A. von Hirsch, *Doing Justice: The Choice of Punishments*, New York, Hill & Wang, 1976. The latter, a report of a Commission which was set up to reform the U.S. system of indeterminate sentences, was based on three related principles: (a) *just deserts* (defendant must be punished as he "deserves," according to his criminal record and gravity of offense); (b) *proportionality* (sentence must be leveled with gravity of offense); (c) *equality* (similar cases must be treated alike). The aim was to eliminate the arbitrariness of indeterminate sentences and to come to a fairer and more just

sentencing policy; accordingly, the judge's discretionary powers were to be restrained, and imprisonment limited to the most serious crimes.

8. Josine Junger-Tas, *Alternatives to Prison Sentences: Experiences and Developments*, Amsterdam, Kugler Publications, 1994, pp. 3-4.

9. Other theorists do mention incapacitation, rehabilitation, individual deterrence, general deterrence, and revenge (Daniel Glaser, "Alternatives to incarceration," in: *International Review of Criminal Policy*, 1980, 36, p. 57).

10. Gerhard O. W. Mueller, *Sentencing: Process and Purpose*, Springfield, Charles Thomas Publisher, 1977; M. Clinard, A. Abbot, *Crime in Developing Countries. A Comparative Perspective*, New York, John Wiley & Sons, 1973; B. Alper, *Prisons Inside-Out: Alternative in Correctional Reform*, Cambridge MA, Ballinger Publishing Company, 1974.

11. The table is neither exhaustive nor conceptually bound to any particular legal system, but rather illustrates the key moments of any criminal justice process. A uniform terminology is difficult to use, given the variety of legal systems worldwide. Some alternatives are used as accessories or extensions to imprisonment, while others are substitutes or sanctions on their own.

CHAPTER 2: THE CIVIL LAW SYSTEM

1. Robert Schmelck, Georges Picca, *Penologie et droit penitentiaire*, Paris, Editions Cujas, 1967, p. 219.

2. Luigi Daga, "Differentes formules penales visant a remplacer la privation de liberte dans les systemes juridiques europeens," in: *Revue internationale de criminologie et de police technique*, Geneve, 1984, April-June, p. 186.

3. J. G. Lopes, "Le traitement des jeunes adultes delinquants au Portugal," in: *Boletim da Administracao Penitenciaria*, 1965, 16, p. 20.

4. Marc Ancel, *Suspended Sentence*, London, Heinemann, 1971, pp. 60-63.

5. Ahmed Lourdjane, "La probation en France," in: *Revue penitentiaire et de droit penal*, 1977, 1, pp. 44-46.

6. M. Ancel, *supra 4*, pp. 65ff.; Renato Breda, "Italy," in: C. G. Cartledge, P. J. P. Tak, M. Tomic-Malic, *Probation in Europe*, Hertogenbosch, The

Netherlands, The European Assembly for Probation and After-care, 1981, pp. 188-190; Thelma Wilson, Paul van Aerschot, Muriel Hammond (eds.), *Prison and Probation Service Compared in Finland, England and Wales*, London, North East London Polytechnic, 1983, pp. 12-26; L. Daga, *supra 2*, pp. 188-190; Kathrin Dorin, "Probation Work in Germany", paper presented at: *Probation in Europe*, symposium, Manchester, 1995, 1-6 May.

7. Stanislaw Frankowski, Eleonora Zielinska, "Non-custodial Penal Measures in European Socialist Countries," in: *International Review of Criminal Policy*, New York, 1980, 36, p. 38.

8. Bela Busch, Jozsef Molnar, Eva Margitan, "Criminal Law, the Law of Criminal Procedure, and the Law of Corrections in Hungary," in: Stanislaw Frankowski, Paul B. Stephan (eds.), *Legal Reform in Post-Communist Europe: The View from Within*, Dordrecht, Martinus Nijhoff Publishers, 1995, p. 240.

9. Andrzej Wasek, Stanislaw Frankowski, "Polish Criminal Law and Procedure," in: S. Frankowski, P. B. Stephan, *supra 8*, p. 277.

10. B. Busch, J. Molnar, E. Margitan, *supra 8*, p. 240.

11. Tiberiu Dianu, "The Romanian Criminal Justice System," in: S. Frankowski, P. B. Stephan, *supra 8*, pp. 262-263.

12. Alexander S. Mikhlin, "The Law of Corrections in Russia," in: S. Frankowski, P. B. Stephan, *supra 8*, p. 339.

13. Currently, a pro-Western regime, resulting from the November 1996 elections, is dealing with a new land reform plan.

14. A. S. Mikhlin, *supra 12*, p. 339.

15. Ioan G. Mihuta, *Condamnarea conditionala*, Bucharest, 1937, pp. 58-61.

16. S. Frankowski, E. Zielinska, *supra 7*, p. 41.

17. A. Wasek, S. Frankowski, *supra 9*, pp. 277, 290; S. Frankowski, E. Zielinska, *supra 7*, p. 42.

18. A. S. Mikhlin, *supra 12*, p. 338.

19. Tiberiu Dianu, "The Evolution of Capital Punishment in Romania," in: *Revue Roumaine des Sciences Juridiques*, 1995, 2, pp. 185-186.

20. Tiberiu Dianu, "Suspendarea conditionata in sistemul Legii nr. 104/1992," in: *Pro Lege*, Bucharest, Public Ministry, 1995, 1, pp. 16-23. see also: *Romania Libera* (Bucharest), August 26, 1997 and October 16, 1997.

21. Rodica-Mihaela Stanoiu, Tiberiu Dianu, "Reform Movements in Criminal Procedure and the Protection of Human Rights," in: *Revue Roumaine des Sciences Juridiques*, 1992, 2, p. 191.

22. A. S. Mikhlin, *supra 12*, pp. 337-338.

23. Comisia Nationala de Statistica, *Anuarul Statistic al Romaniei 1994*, Bucharest, 1995, pp. 696-697; T. Dianu, *supra 19*, p. 187.

24. B. Busch, J. Molnar, E. Margitan, *supra 8*, p. 240.

25. J. Enrique Castillo Barrantes, "Prison Substitutes: Present Status and Trends in Latin America," in: *International Review of Criminal Policy*, New York, 1980, 36, p. 48.

26. Carlos Fontan Balestra, *Derecho Penal: Parte General*, Buenos Aires, Abeledo-Perrot, 1974, pp. 643-644.

27. Ruy Carose de Mello Fucunduva, "A prisao-albergue e a crise do sistema penitenciario," in: *Justitia*, Sao Paulo, 1976, 4, p. 45.

28. Silvia Pena Wasaff, "Modificaciones a la ley chilena de condena condicional," in: *Revista de Ciencias Juridicas*, Valparaiso, 1973, 4, p. 135.

29. Luiz Pereira de Melo, "Patronatos dos Liberados e Egressos das Prisoes," in: *Revista do Conselho Penitenciario do Distrito Federal*, Brasilia, 1969, 1, p. 51; Juan B. Vitale Nocera, "El organismo tecnico-criminologico exigido por la ley penitenciaria nacional," in: *Revista de Derecho Penal y Criminologia*, Buenos Aires, 1969, 3, p. 361; Jose M. Rico, *Crimen y Justicia en America Latina*, Ciudad de Mexico, Siglo XXI, 1977, p. 375; J. E. Castillo Barrantes, *supra 25*, p. 49.

CHAPTER 3: THE COMMON LAW SYSTEM

1. Bail was quickly adopted by some post-Communist countries. Romania, for instance, implemented two models, both of Western origin: regular bail and bail with supervision (by Law 32 of 1990 and Law 45 of 1993).

2. R. J. Walker, *The English Legal System*, London, Butterworths, 1985, p. 467; NACRO, *Pre-Trial Initiatives Paper 1: Bail Support. Some Considerations of Current Policy and Practice*, London, 1993, p. 1; NACRO, *Pre-Trial Initiatives Paper 4: Making an assessment for a bail support service. The role of assessment guidance*, London, 1994, p. 1; NACRO, *The*

Bail (Amendment) Act 1993, London, 1994, pp. 1-3; NACRO, *The Criminal Justice and Public Order Act 1994 and Bail*, London, 1994, p. 1.

3. From a Home Office investigation it appears that in projects directed at juveniles whose cases has been dropped, 57% of the young people involved attempted to give the victim an explanation of their behavior and apologized; compensation was paid in about 25% cases, and in some cases work was done for the victim; 80% of the victims of juvenile crime and 50% of the victims of adults were prepared to cooperate (T. F. Marshall, "Victim-Offender Mediation," in: *Home Office Research Bulletin*, 1991, 30).

4. John Pritchard, *The Penguin Guide to the Law*, Harmondsworth, Middlesex, Penguin Books, 1984, pp. 801-802.

5. Andrew Ashworth, *Sentencing and Criminal Justice*, London, Weidenfeld & Nicolson, 1992, p. 248.

6. Home Office, *Alternatives to Short Terms of Imprisonment. Report of the Advisory Council on the Treatment of Offenders*, London, HMSO, 1957, pp. 8-9, 18; R. Morgan, R. Bowles, *Fines Project*, Home Office Interim Report, 1981, unpublished; J. Pritchard, *supra 4*, pp. 799-800; N. Moss, *Tackling Fine Default*, London, Prison Reform Trust, 1989; Stephen Shaw, "Monetary penalties and imprisonment: the realistic alternatives," in: Pat Carlen, Dee Cook (eds.), *Paying for Crime*, Milton Keynes, Open University Press, 1989, pp. 34-35; Greater Manchester Probation Service, *Money Payment Supervision Order*, Manchester, 1993; Gordon C. Barclay, *Criminal Justice System in England and Wales*, London, Home Office, 1995, p. 27.

7. A system of unit fines was introduced in magistrates' courts by *The Criminal Justice Act 1991*, s. 18, Chapter 53, but due to difficulties, the system was abolished by *The Criminal Justice Act 1993*, s. 65. *The CJA 1993* required that all courts should set fines reflecting the seriousness of the offense and the offender's financial capabilities; see also Josine Junger-Tas, *Alternatives to Prison Sentences. Experiences and Developments*, Amsterdam, Kugler Publications, 1994, pp. 22-24; G. C. Barclay, *supra 6*, p. 27.

8. Home Office, *supra 6*, pp. 9, 26.

9. In 1967, suspended sentence was designed as a substitute for imprisonment, but courts began to use it as an alternative to other non-custodial devices, such as fine or probation. After a decade of constant criticism, it was reported that "if the main object of the suspended sentence

was to reduce the prison population, there are considerable doubts as to whether it has achieved this effect" (Advisory Council on the Penal System, *Sentences of Imprisonment*, London, HMSO, 1978, p. 117); see also, A. E. Bottoms, "The Suspended Sentence in England 1967-1978," in: *British Journal of Criminology*, 1981, 21, pp. 1-26; Antony A. Vass, *Alternatives to Prison: Punishment, Custody and the Community*, London, Sage Publications, 1990, pp. 80-81; A. Ashworth, *supra 5*, pp. 274-275.

10. A. Ashworth, *supra 5*, p. 277.

11. Nigel Stone, "The Suspended Sentence since the Criminal Justice Act 1991," in: *The Criminal Law Review*, 1994, June, p. 399.

12. Home Office, "Criminal Appeals: England and Wales - 1992," in: *Home Office Statistical Bulletin*, 1994, 1.

13. Home Office, *Non-Custodial and Semi-Custodial Penalties: Report of the Advisory Council on the Penal System*, London, HMSO, 1970, p. 68; Home Office, *The Sentence of the Court: A Handbook for Courts on the Treatment of Offenders*, London, HMSO, 1978, p. 23; R. J. Walker, *The English Legal System*, London, Butterworths, 1985, pp. 522-523; Martin Wasik, *Emmins on Sentencing*, London, Blackstone Press, 1993, p. 197; Greater Manchester & District, *Greater Manchester - Attendance Centers*, Manchester, 1993, pp. 4-7.

14. Stuart Vernon, *Social Work and the Law*, London, Butterworths, 1993, p. 164; M. Wasik, *supra 13*, pp. 200-207; G. C. Barclay, *supra 6*, pp. 25-26.

15. Home Office, *Circular 30 of 1992*, par. 9; Home Office, Department of Health, Welsh Office, *National Standards for the Supervision of Offenders in the Community 1992*, London, Home Office Probation Service Division, 1992, p. 51.

16. *The Children and Young Persons Act 1933* (s. 44) set out the principle that all courts must have regard for the welfare of the child or young person who appears before them; *The CJA 1991* brought 17-year-old offenders within the scope of this provision; *National Standards 1992* (s. 4.1) made it clear that the younger the offender the more important the welfare requirement is, whereas *National Standards 1995* recommended that the standard should apply to all ages for which a supervision order is available to the courts (Home Office, Department of Health, Welsh Office, *National Standards for*

the Supervision of Offenders in the Community 1995, London, Home Office Probation Service Division, 1995, p. 24).

17. E.g., in Liverpool, the South Knowsley Probation Center organized group sessions, where individuals have a stronger feeling of security, and inter-communication becomes more active; the sessions replaced the former probation set-ups, somewhat intimidating for clients; see Home Office, *Facing Up to Crime: The Changing World of Probation Work*, London, Home Office Public Relations Branch, 1993, pp. 8-9.

18. Probation officers are often reluctant to recommend and use night restriction orders in court. Such a "surveillance" type is deemed as diverging from the original social work functions and the requirements imposed are seldom applicable; see also *infra*, "(e.6) Curfew orders."

19. *National Standards 1995, supra 16*, p. 17.

20. *The PCCA 1973*, Schedule 1A, Par. 3, as inserted by *The CJA 1991*, Sch. I, Part II, imposed attendance to probation center as a further requirement to be specified in probation orders. Paragraph 3(3)(a) fixed a 60-day period for attending the center, extendible, as Paragraph 4(1) put it, to the maximum duration of a probation order, in case of sex offenders. Government instructions require more demanding probation orders than in the past, when the device was seen by some as a "soft option" (see M. Wasik, *supra 13*, p. 173). Assumably, probation centers will impose stricter programs for serious offenders, although both legislation and government standards leave room for enough flexibility regarding the intensity and the type of program applicable; see *National Standards 1992, supra 15*, p. 45.

21. Between 1973 and 1974, community service schemes were initiated in six experimental areas (Home Office, "Community Service Orders," in: *Home Office Research Study*, 1975, 29), and their number increased after 1975. Probation and after-care committees have prerogatives in organizing the schemes in accordance with local conditions.

22. A. Willis, "Community Service as an Alternative to Imprisonment: A Cautionary View," in: *Probation Journal*, 1977, 24, pp. 120-126; W. Young, *Community Service Orders: The Development and Use of a New Penal Measure*, London, Heinemann, 1979; Ken Pease, "Community Service and Prison: Are They Alternatives?," in: Ken Pease, W. McWilliams (eds.), *Community Service by Order*, Edinburgh, Scottish Academic Press, 1980, pp. 27-42; Antony A. Vass, "Community Service for Juveniles? A Critical

Comment," in: *Probation Journal*, 1981, 28, pp. 44-49; J. Andrews, *Alternatives to Custody: A Study of Social Inquiry Reports*, Manchester, Greater Manchester Probation and After-care Service Information Unit, 1982; Ken Pease, "Community Service as an Alternative to Custody (I)," in: *Community Service Newsletter*, 1986, 15, pp. 15-18; K. Pease, "Community Service as an Alternative to Custody (II)," in: *Community Service Newsletter*, 1986, 16, pp. 3-6; Antony A. Vass, "Community Service: Areas of Concern and Suggestions for Change," in: *Howard Journal of Criminal Justice*, 1986, 25, pp. 100-111; A. A. Vass, *supra 9*, pp. 82-85. The lack of clear guidance and the failure of the Court of Appeal to supply it made the English sentencers determined to find certain agreed "scales of equivalence" between detention and the number of hours for community service (e.g., 190 hours = 9 months), or to draw distinctions between an order of 100 hours or longer, regarded as "alternatives to custody" and another one of up to 100 hours, regarded as being imposed "as a sentence in its own right;" see also A. Ashworth, *supra 5*, p. 269, and M. Wasik, *supra 13*, p. 185. These distinctions are difficult to match to the structure of *The CJA 1991*, in which the rhetoric of "alternatives to custody" has been abandoned.

23. Research data showed that prison records and age have little relevance on the duration of community service; also, the type of offense, the number of previous convictions and the number of previous detentions had equally little effect on the length of the sanction. A variable with constant influence is the offender's occupation: the unemployed get longer orders than the employed, which may lead to crime inflation; see also Ken Pease, "Community Service Orders," in: Michael Tonry, Norval Morris (eds.), *Crime and Justice: An Annual Review of Research*, Chicago, University of Chicago Press, 1985.

24. *National Standards 1995*, *supra 16*, p. 34; Greater Manchester Probation Service, *Community Service Order*, Manchester, 1993, p. 2.

25. E.g., in the *Eric Cantona* case, the offender was ordered to perform 120 hours of community service working with aspiring young footballers (*The Times*, 1995, April 1, p. 3).

26. K. Pease, P. Durkin, I. Earnshaw, D. Payne, J. Thorpe, "Community Service Orders," in: *Home Office Research Studies*, 1975, 29, p. 70; A. Ashworth, *supra 5*, p. 268.

27. C. D. Skinns, "Community Service Practice," in: *British Journal of Criminology*, 1990, 1. Some courts imposed four times more community

service orders than others; about 65% of orders were imposed for offenses against property, and 25% for traffic offenses; 35% of those doing community service were previously detained; the average order length was 140 hours (K. Pease, *supra 23*).

28. *The National Standards* have led to an increase of orders terminated for breach of conditions (from 14% in 1988 to 17% in 1989), which, in turn, increased the number of convictions for the breach of order. Until 1990, the number of both completed and breached community service orders increased significantly. Breach procedure is usually triggered after three (initially, four) unexplained absences, but preserve the probation officer's discretion not to return the offender to court in "usual and exceptional" circumstances; see also Charles Lloyd, "National Standards for Community Service Orders: The First Two Years of Operation," in: *Home Office Research Bulletin*, 1991, 31; A. Ashworth, *supra 5*, pp. 268-269.

29. Cedric Fullwood (Chief Probation Officer, Greater Manchester Probation Service), *discussion with author*, Manchester, May 1, 1995.

30. M. Wasik, *supra 13*, p. 187;

31. *National Standards 1995, supra 16*, p. 41.

32. *National Standards 1992, supra 15*, p. 81.

33. A. Ashworth, *supra 5*, p. 272.

34. HM Inspectorate of Probation, 1993, cf. M. Wasik, *supra 13*, p. 189.

35. A. Ashworth, *supra 5*, p. 265.

36. Hugh Marriage (Home Office, Probation Division), *discussion with author*, London, May 19, 1995.

37. Philip Lloyd (Probation Office, Greater Manchester Probation Service), *discussion with author*, Manchester, May 5, 1995; C. Fullwood, *supra 29*.

38. The Rt. Hon. The Lord Carlisle of Bucklow QC (Chairman), *The Parole System in England and Wales: Report of the Review Committee*, London, HMSO, 1988.

39. Roger Hood, Stephen Shute, *Parole in Transition: Evaluating the Impact and Effects of Changes in the Parole System*, Oxford, University of Oxford, Center for Criminological Research, 1994, pp. 88-89.

40. Steven H. Gifis, *Law Dictionary*, New York, Barron's Educational Series, Inc., 1991, pp. 38, 134-135, 369, 407.

41. J. Galvin et al., *Instead of Jails*, Washington, National Institute of Law Enforcement and Criminal Justice of the United States Department of Justice, 1977.

42. C. Shelbourn, "Compensation for Detention," in: *Criminal Law Review*, 1978, 2.

43. Burt Gallaway, Joe Hudson, *Criminal Justice, Restitution, and Reconciliation*, New York, Criminal Justice Press, 1990; Robert Carter, Jay Cocks, Daniel Glaser, "Community Service: A Review of the Basic Issues," in: *Federal Probation*, 1987, LI, pp. 4-11.

44. Joseph J. Senna, Larry J. Siegel, *Introduction to Criminal Justice*, St. Paul MN, West Publishing Company, 1993, p. 546.

45. Peter R. Schneider, William R. Griffith, Anne L. Schneider, "Juvenile Restitution As a Sole Sanction or Condition of Probation: An Empirical Analysis," in: *Journal of Research in Crime and Delinquency*, 1982, 1, pp. 47-63 (a study on 10,000 juvenile court cases revealing the higher success rate for completing restitution orders alone compared with restitution as a condition for probation).

46. Frederick Allen, Harvey Treger, "Community Service Orders in Federal Probation: Perceptions of Probationers and Host Agencies," in: *Federal Probation*, 1990, LIV, pp. 8-14.

47. Peter Schneider, Anne Schneider, William Griffith, *Monthly Report of the National Juvenile Restitution Evaluation Project V*, Eugene OR, Institute for Policy Analysis, 1981.

48. Anne Schneider, "Restitution and Recidivism Rates of Juvenile Offenders: Four Experimental Studies," in: *Criminology*, 1986, 24, pp. 533-552.

49. James Austin, Barry Krisberg, "The Unmet Promise of Alternatives to Incarceration," in: *Crime and Delinquency*, 1982, 28, pp. 374-409; Alan Harland, "Court-Ordered Community Service in Criminal Law: The Continuing Tyranny of Benevolence," in: *Buffalo Law Review*, 1980, Summer, pp. 425-486.

50. J. P. Conrad, "News of the Future: Research and Developments in Corrections," in: *Federal Probation*, 1988, 3, pp. 1-2.

51. E.g., The Boston *Crime and Justice Foundation* (Massachusetts), associated with the Lawyers' Union, supplied most of the voluntary staff; it successfully cooperated with the Judiciary, which referred 90% of the cases to

its projects (F. Zeder, *La mediation penale: phenomene marginal ou prometteur?*, Paris, Universite de Loi, Economie et Sciences Sociales, 1990, September).

52. E.g., in the *Ivan Boeski* case, the defendant paid over US$ 100 million for violating insider stock trading rules; in the *Drexel Burnham Lambert* case, the firm-defendant paid a $650 million fine for security violations (David Pauly, Carolyn Friday, "Drexel's Crumbling Defense," in: *Newsweek*, 1988, December 19, p. 44).

53. George Cole, Barry Mahoney, Marlene Thorton, Roger Hanson, *The Practices and Attitudes of Trial Court Judges Regarding Fines as a Criminal Sanction*, Washington, DC, U.S. Government Printing Office, 1987.

54. Norval Morris, Michael Tonry, *Between Prison and Probation: Intermediate Punishments in a Rational Sentencing System*, New York, Oxford University Press, 1990, p. 90. Yet many other courts ordered custody for noncompliance with financial orders. Also, the U.S. Supreme Court ruled out that putting those unable to pay fines in custody is a discriminatory practice against the poor; see Tate v. Short (1971), 401 U.S. 395.

55. J. Junger-Tas, *supra 7*, p. 24.

56. E.g., in Texas, 80% of the imposed fines originate from this type of contribution, which makes up 50% of the Department of Adult Probation budget; see G. R. Wheeler, R. V. Hissong, M. P. Slusher, T. M. Macan, "Economic Sanctions in Criminal Justice: Dilemma for Human Service?," in: *Justice System Journal*, 1990, 14, pp. 63-77.

57. E.g., in Texas (Harris County), drunk drivers are assessed the cost of the videotape used to record their behavior; see George F. Cole, Monetary Sanctions: "The Problem of Compliance," in: James M. Byrne, Arthur J. Lurigio, Joan Petersilia (eds.), *Smart Sentencing: The Emergence of Intermediate Sanctions*, Newbury Park, Sage Publications, 1992, p. 143.

58. The quantum of a fine is fixed according to the seriousness of the crime committed, the income level, the number of dependents and other factors quantified on a chart similar to the income-tax table (Wade Lambert, "Three States, Seeking Alternatives to Jail, Will Test Fines Tied to Criminals' Income," in: *Wall Street Journal*, 1991, December 12, p. 1B).

59. Margaret Gordon, Daniel Glaser, "The Use and Effects of Financial Penalties in Municipal Courts," in : *Criminology*, 1991, 29, pp. 651-676.

60. J. J. Senna, L. J. Siegel, *supra 44*, p. 545.

61. E.g., seizing million-dollar yachts for small amounts of marijuana found aboard. Both these confiscatory practices, arbitrary in nature, referred to as "zero tolerance," and the administration which promoted such victimizing policies, were criticized; see David Fried, "Rationalizing Criminal Forfeiture," in: *Journal of Criminal Law and Criminology*, 1988, 79, p. 436.

62. J. J. Senna, L. J. Siegel, *supra 44*, p. 553.

63. E.g., the residential community corrections facilities are considered a correctional alternative halfway between traditional probation and custody. Placement in such a center can be a probation requirement for offenders in need of a non-secure community facility with a more structured treatment environment than that of classical probation.

64. Jack McDevitt, Robyn Miliano, "Day Reporting Centers: An Innovative Concept in Intermediate Sanctions," in: J. M. Byrne, A. J. Lurigio, J. Petersilia, *supra 57*, pp. 152-165.

65. For the Anglo-American probation system, see Chapters 7 to 10.

66. See also Chapters 11 and 12.

67. Paul Friday, *International Probation*, Washington, National Institute of Law Enforcement and Criminal Justice of the United States Department of Justice, 1979; H. Allen et al., *Critical Issues in Adult Probation*, Washington, National Institute of Law Enforcement and Criminal Justice of the United States Department of Justice, 1979.

68. Chief Probation Officers of California, *Probation Standards*, San Bernardino CA, 1980.

69. Norval Morris, "Alternatives to Imprisonment: Failures and Prospects," in: *Criminal Justice Research Bulletin* (Houston TX), 1987, 7; N. Morris, M. Tonry, *supra 54*, pp. 154-158.

70. Parole is normally associated with indeterminate sentence yet post-imprisonment supervision and care can also be ordered in a fixed sentence scheme.

71. American Friends' Service Committee, *Struggle for Justice*, New York, Hill & Wang, 1971.

72. J. Kress, L. Wilkins, D. Gottfredson, "Is the End of Judicial Sentencing in Sight?," in: *Judicature*, 1976, 60.

73. Norval Morris, *The Future of Imprisonment*, Chicago, University of Chicago Press, 1974; A. von Hirsch, *Doing Justice: The Choice of Punishments*, New York, Hill & Wang, 1976.

74. J. Potter, "Annual Prison Population Survey: Growth Slow - At Least for Now," in: *Corrections Magazine*, 1979, April.

75. Law Reform Commission of Canada, *Restitution and Compensation*, Ottawa, 1976.

76. M. Jackson, J. Ekstedt, *Alternatives to Incarceration - Sentencing Option Programs: What Are the Alternatives?*, Research Report of the Canadian Sentencing Commission, Ottawa, Department of Justice, 1988.

77. J. McKay, M. Rook, *The Work-Order Scheme: An Evaluation of Tasmania's Work-Order Scheme*, Hobart (Australia), 1976; I. Potas, "Alternatives to Imprisonment," in: D. Biles (ed.), *Crime and Justice in Australia*, Canberra, Australian Institute of Criminology, 1977.

78. P. Ward, "Weekend Detention," in: *Australian and New Zealand Journal of Criminology*, 1969, 4; E. Missen, "Periodic Detention in New Zealand," in: *Resource Material Series*, United Nations Asia and Far East Institute for the Prevention of Crime and the Treatment of Offenders, 1975, 11; M. Stace, "Periodic Detention Work Centers," in: *Australian and New Zealand Journal of Criminology*, 1979, 2.

79. Kare Tonnesen, *Uso de alternativas a la reclusion en cuatro diferentes paises: Costa Rica, Venezuela, Peru y Jamaica*, San Jose, Costa Rica, United Nations Latin American Institute for the Prevention of Crime and Treatment of Offenders (ILANUD), 1979; *Jamaica Gazette - Supplement: Bills and Acts*, vol. C, 1977, June 17, no. 13.

80. D. Allen, "Increasing Community Involvement in the Treatment of Offenders in Jamaica," in: *Social Defense*, 1977, April.

CHAPTER 4: OTHER LEGAL SYSTEMS

1. M. Zeid, "Alternatives to Imprisonment: Note on the Arab Region," in: *International Review of Criminal Policy*, 1980, 36, p. 59.

2. United Nations Asia and Far East Institute for the Prevention of Crime and the Treatment of Offenders (UNAFEI), "Alternatives to Imprisonment in Asia," in: *International Review of Criminal Policy*, 1980, 36, pp. 27-37.

3. The rehabilitative potential of open treatment has come to the attention of the public and administrators. At the Iwahig Penal Colony (the Philippines), colonists can bring their families, at Government expense, to

live and work in the colony, they get paid for overtime, and after release they can be allotted a piece of land in the neighborhood to settle down permanently (UNAFEI, *supra 2*, p. 34).

4. A. Milner (ed.), *African Penal Systems*, New York, Praeger, 1969, p. 30.

5. R. B. Seldman, J. D. Abaka Eylson, "Ghana," in: A. Milner, *supra 4*, p. 83; The Prison Department of Nigeria, *Annual Report: 1958-1959*, Section 82; J. S. Read, "Kenya, Tanzania and Uganda," in: A. Milner, *supra 4*.

6. James S. E. Opolot, "Alternatives to Imprisonment in the New States of Africa," in: *International Review of Criminal Policy*, 1980, 36, pp. 25-26.

CHAPTER 5: PROBATION AND SUSPENDED SENTENCE: PROS AND CONS

1. United Nations, *Practical Results and Financial Aspects of Adult Probation in Selected Countries*, New York, Department of Social Affairs, Division of Social Welfare, 1954, p. 1.

2. United Nations, *European Seminar on Probation*, London, 20-30 October 1952, see "National statements" of Belgium and France; Marie-Francoise Petit, Jean-Pierre Robert, "France," in: C. G. Cartledge, P. J. P. Tak, M. Tomic-Malic, *Probation in Europe*, Hertogenbosch, The Netherlands, The European Assembly for Probation and After-care, 1981, p. 96.

3. Max Grunhut, "Probation in Germany," in: *Howard Journal*, 1952, 8, pp. 168-174; Alfons Wahl, "Germany," in: C. G. Cartledge, P. J. P. Tak, M. Tomic-Malic, *supra 2*, p. 132.

4. Roger Tanner (Manager, National Association for the Care and Resettlement of Offenders-NACRO, Greater Manchester New Careers Training), *interview with author*, February 9, 1995; Tom Stanway (Probation Officer, Probation Service Christian Fellowship, Ashbourne, Derbyshire), *discussion with author*, Market Harborough, Leicestershire, June 15, 1995.

5. For France, see Marc Ancel, *Suspended Sentence*, London, Heinemann, 1971, pp. 58-59.

6. E.g., in Romania, courts use the standard no-supervision suspended sentence in 95% of the cases, and conditional sentence (introduced by Law

104 of 1992) in only 5% of the cases (Comisia Nationala de Statistica, *Anuarul Statistic al Romaniei 1994*, Bucharest, 1995, p. 697).

7. Tiberiu Dianu, *Evolutia suspendarii executarii pedepsei*, in manuscript, Bucharest, 1994, pp. 41-43.

8. M. Ancel, *supra 5*, pp. 66-67.

CHAPTER 6: LEGAL NATURE AND FUNCTIONS

1. *The Probation of Offenders Act 1907* classified probation and discharge in the same section, giving credit to the idea of a new "let off" for offenders.

2. Max Grunhut, *The Selection of Offenders for Probation*, New York, United Nations, 1959. *The Criminal Justice Act 1948* classified probation in a separate section, and the court was required to decide upon an order of absolute or conditional discharge only after it satisfied itself that punishment was not expedient and the probation order was not appropriate.

3. Joan F. S. King, *The Probation and After-Care Service*, London, Butterworths, 1969, pp. 8-9.

4. Elizabeth R. Glover, *Probation and Re-education*, London, Routledge & Kegan Paul Limited, 1956, p. 25.

5. Kent Probation and After-Care Service, *Probation Control Unit: A Community Based Experiment in Intensive Supervision*, Annual Report on the Work of the Medway Center, Maidstone, Medway, 1981; Peter Raynor, *Social Work, Justice and Control*, Oxford, Basil Blackwell, 1985, p. 47.

6. Roger Tanner (NACRO Manchester), *interview with author*, February 9, 1995; Bob Broad, *Punishment Under Pressure: The Probation Service in the Inner City*, London, Jessica Kingsley Publishers, 1991, p. 20.

7. Home Office, *Punishment, Custody and the Community* (Cmd 424), London, HMSO, 1988; Home Office, *Crime, Justice and Protecting the Public. The Government's Proposals for Legislation* (Cmnd 965), London, HMSO, 1990.

8. Digby Anderson, "Jail: The Random Punishment," in: *Sunday Telegraph*, 1989, February 5; Editorial, "Law Reform Set to Curb Jailing", in: *The Guardian*, 1990, 2 January.

9. Bill McWilliams, "Community Service National Standards: Practice and Sentencing," in: *Probation Journal*, 1989, 3, pp. 125-126.

10. R. A. Duff, "Punishment in the Community: A Philosophical Perspective," in: Huw Rees, Eryl Hall Williams (eds.), *Punishment, Custody and the Community. Reflections and Comments on the Green Paper*, London, London School of Economics and Political Science, 1989, pp. 136-139, 149-150; David Garland, "Critical Reflections on the Green Paper," in: H. Rees, E. Hall Williams, *ibid.*, p. 8.

11. T. Palmer, "Martinson Revisited," in: *Journal of Research in Crime and Delinquency*, 1975, 12, p. 133; S. R. Brody, "The Effectiveness of Sentencing: A Review of the Literature," in: *Home Office Research Unit Report*, London, HMSO, 1976, 35; D. J. Rothman, *Conscience and Convenience: The Asylum and its Alternatives in Progressive America*, Boston, Little Brown, 1980; A. Scull, "Community Corrections: Panacea, Progress or Pretense," in: David Garland, P. Young (eds.), *The Power to Punish: Contemporary Penality and Social Analysis*, London, Heinemann, 1983, pp. 146-165.

12. American Friends' Service Committee, *Struggle for Justice*, New York, Hill & Wang, 1971; D. Fogel, *The Justice Model for Corrections*, Cincinnati OH, Anderson, 1975; A. von Hirsch, *Doing Justice: The Choice of Punishments*, New York, Hill & Wang, 1976.

13. E. van den Haag, *Punishing Criminals: On an Old and Painful Question*, New York, Basic Books, 1975; J. Q. Wilson, *Thinking about Crime*, New York, Basic Books, 1975.

14. Douglas R. Thomson, "The Changing Face of Probation in the USA," in: John Harding, *Probation and the Community: A Practice and Policy Reader*, London, Tavistock Publications, 1987, p. 102.

15. Robert Martinson, "What Works? Questions and Answers about Prison Reform," in: *The Public Interest*, 1974, 35, pp. 303-309; Douglas Lipton, Robert Martinson, Judith Wilks, *The Effectiveness of Correctional Treatment: A Survey of Treatment Evaluation Studies*, New York, Praeger, 1975 (focus on 231 correctional program evaluations produced between 1945-1967 outlining the low impact of the rehabilitative efforts on recidivism).

16. Robert R. Ross, Paul Gendreau, *Effective Correctional Treatment*, Toronto, Butterworths, 1980.

17. In 1982, only 44% subjects identified rehabilitation as the most preferred "main emphasis" in prisons (compared with 73% in 1970); see E. J. Brown, T. J. Flanagan, M. McLeod, eds., *Sourcebook of Criminal Justice Statistics 1983*, Washington DC, U.S. Department of Justice, Bureau of Justice Statistics, 1984, p. 261).

18. J. F. O'Connor, *The Fiscal Crisis of the State*, New York, St. Martin's Press, 1973; A. T. Scull, *Decarceration: Community Treatment and the Deviant. A Radical View*, Englewood Cliffs NJ, Prentice-Hall, 1977; F. A. Allen, *The Decline of the Rehabilitative Ideal: Penal Policy and Social Purpose*, New Haven CT, Yale University Press, 1981; F. Cullen, J. Wozniak, "Fighting the Appeal of Repression," in: *Crime and Social Justice*, 1982, 18, pp. 23-33.

19. E. Pashukanis, *Law and Marxism: A General Theory*, London, Ink Links, 1978; J. H. Reiman, S. Headlee, "Marxism and Criminal Justice Policy," in: *Crime and Delinquency*, 1981, 1, pp. 24-47.

20. D. Clemmer, *The Prison Community*, Quincy MA, Christopher, 1940; M. N. Zald, "Power Balance and Staff Conflict in Correctional Institutions," in: *Administrative Science Quarterly*, 1962, 7, pp. 22-49; M. N. Zald, "Organizational Control Structure in Five Correctional Institutions," in: *American Journal of Sociology*, 1962, 68, pp. 335-345; J. R. Hepburn, C. Albonetti, "Role Conflict in Correctional Institutions: An Empirical Examination of the Treatment-Custody Dilemma Among Correctional Staff," in: *Criminology*, 1980, 4, pp. 445-459.

21. P. M. Harris, T. R. Clear, S. C. Baird, "Have Community Service Officers Changed Their Attitude Toward Their Work?," in: *Justice Quarterly*, 1989, 2, pp. 233-246.

22. Thomas Ellsworth, "Identifying the Actual and Preferred Goals of Adult Probation," in: *Federal Probation*, 1990, 2, pp. 10-15 (among the 30 most important statements for the adult probation system, 512 respondents identified 17 items as reflecting enforcement practices and 13 as reflecting rehabilitation practices; the relatively balanced distribution led to the conclusion that probation staff view probation goals as equally focused on both enforcement and rehabilitation).

23. Koichi Hamai, Renaud Ville, "Origins and Purpose of Probation," in: Koichi Hamai, Renaud Ville, Robert Harris, Mike Hough, Ugljesa Zvekic

(eds.), *Probation Round the World: A Comparative Study*, London, Routledge, 1995, pp. 72, 83.

24. R. Foren, R. Bailey, *Authority in Social Casework*, Oxford, Pergamon Press, 1968; Robert J. Harris, "The Probation Officer As a Social Worker," in: *British Journal of Social Work*, 1977, 4; Robert J. Harris, "A Changing Service: The Case for Separating Care and Control in Probation Practice," in: *British Journal of Social Work*, 1980; Mike Hough, "Variations in Probation Function," in: K. Hamai et al., *supra 23*, pp. 161-173.

25. Peter Raynor, *Social Work, Justice and Control*, Oxford, Basil Blackwell, 1985, p. 46.

26. N. Morris, *The Future of Imprisonment*, Chicago IL, University of Chicago Press, 1974; Jenny Roberts, "Probation in the Criminal and Civil Justice Systems," in: Association of Chief Officers of Probation, *Probation in Focus*, Westminster, ACOP, 1993, p. 9.

27. W. L. Barkdull, "Probation: Call It Control - And Mean It," in: *Federal Probation*, 4, 1976; Harry Joe Jaffe, "Probation with a Flair," in: *Federal Probation*, 1979, 1.

28. D. Burnham, "The New Orthodoxy," in: *Probation Journal*, 1981, 4, p. 1; W. A. Griffiths, "Supervision in the Community," in: *Justice of the Peace*, 1982, August, p. 21.

29. M. Bryant, J. Coker, B. Estlea, S. Himmel, T. Knapp, "Sentenced to Social Work," in: *Probation Journal*, 1978, 4; N. Harlow, E. K. Nelson, *Management Strategies for Probation in an Era of Limits*, Berkeley CA, University of Southern California, Bay Area Research Center, 1982; D. E. Duffee, "Client Biography and Probation Organization," in: P. D. McAnany, D. Thomson, D. Fogel (eds.), *Probation and Justice: Reconsideration of Mission*, Cambridge MA, Oelgeschlager, Gunn & Hain, 1984, Chapter 10.

30. Anthony E. Bottoms, W. McWilliams, "A Non-Treatment Paradigm for Probation Practice," in: *British Journal of Social Work*, 1979, 2; National Association of Probation Officers, *The Provision of Alternatives to Custody and the Use of the Probation Order*, London, NAPO, 1981.

31. J. Q. Wilson, *Varieties of Police Behavior: The Management of Law and Order in Eight Communities*, Cambridge MA, Harvard University Press, 1968; D. E. Duffee, "The Community Context of Probation," in: P. D. McAnany, D. Thomson, D. Fogel, *supra 29*, Chapter 12; E. K. Nelson, L.

Segal, N. Harlow, *Probation Under Fiscal Constraints*, Washington DC, National Institute of Justice, 1984.

32. James McGuire, Philip Priestley, *Offending Behavior: Skills and Strategies for Going Straight*, London, Batsford, 1985; Robert R. Ross, Elizabeth A. Fabiano, *Time to Think: A Cognitive Model of Delinquency Prevention and Rehabilitation*, Ottawa, Institute of Social Sciences and Arts, 1985; Robert R. Ross, Elizabeth A. Fabiano, C. D. Ewles, "Reasoning and Rehabilitation," in: *International Journal of Offender Therapy and Comparative Criminology*, 1988, 20, pp. 165-173.

33. In England and Wales, *The CJA 1991* turned probation into a new type of penalty, while *The Criminal Justice and Public Order Act 1994*, by invoking the heavy caseload awaiting pre-sentence reports, removed their compulsory submission in court. Yet a survey in Greater Manchester area estimated that 70-75% of judges find them essential for the file, cf. Cedric Fullwood, "Criminal Justice and the Role of Community Penalties," paper presented at: *Probation in Europe*, International Symposium, Manchester, May 1-6, 1995. In Canada, Bill C-90, tabled in the House of Commons in July 1992, set out a Statement of the Purpose and Principles of Sentencing that focused on the use of sanctions in the community (K. Hamai, R. Ville, *supra 23*, p. 83).

34. M. Hough, *supra 24*, p. 168.

CHAPTER 7: A HISTORICAL SURVEY

Abbreviations: N.E. = North Eastern Reporter; U.S. = United States Reports.

1. According to Aethelstan's decree, "men should slay none younger than a fifteen winters' man . . . If his kindred will not take him or be surety for him, then swear he as the bishop shall teach him, that he will shun all evil, and let him be in bondage for his price. And if after that he steal, let men slay him or hang him, as they did to his elders" (British Home Office, *Report of the Departmental Committee on the Treatment of Young Offenders*, London, 1927, p. 7).

2. Charles Lionel Chute, Marjorie Bell, *Crime, Courts, and Probation*, New York, The MacMillan Company, 1956, pp. 12-15.

3. William Blackstone, *Commentaries on the Laws of England, 1765-1769*, Albany NY, Banks & Co., 1900, p. 1041.

4. C. L. Chute, M. Bell, *supra 2*, pp. 18-20; Colin H. Roberts, *The Probation Service: History, Structure and Work*, Manchester, University of Manchester Department of Social Administration, 1982, p. 1.

5. L. Le Mesurier (ed.), *Handbook of Probation*, London, National Association of Probation Officers, 1935, p. 23; *The Encyclopedia Britannica*, Vol. XIX, Cambridge, The University Press, 1952, p. 12; Elizabeth A. Martin (ed.), *A Dictionary of Law*, Oxford, Oxford University Press, 1994, p. 329.

6. British Home Office, *supra 1*, p. 10; Dorothy Bochel, *Probation and After-Care: Its Development in England and Wales*, Edinburgh, Scottish Academic Press, 1976, p. 6ff.; Victor A. McLaren, *Perspectives in Probation: Essays in History, Theory and Practice*, Manchester, 1982, p. 4; C. H. Roberts, *supra 4*, p. 1.

7. Matthew Davenport Hill, *Suggestions for the Repression of Crime, Contained in Charges Delivered to Grand Juries of Birmingham*, London, 1857, pp. 601-602.

8. *The Principles of Punishment as Applied in the Administration of the Criminal Law by Judges and Magistrates*, London, 1877, pp. 160-164.

9. The Church of England Temperance Society, established in 1862 as the Church of England Total Abstinence Society, is currently incorporated into the Church of England Council for Social Aid. The early temperance societies were almost exclusively non-conformists and gained little support from either the Anglican Church or from the magistracy. The missionaries were themselves largely from respectable working class origins, practicing schoolteaching, journalism, non-conformist preaching and "teetotal lecturing," believing in the moral elevation of people. In the 1870s, the Society enjoyed tremendous success when the Anglican Church realized that drunkenness was a rival worship to Christianity and temperance provided a means of uniting all Christians against bad mores; see also B. Harrison, *Drink and the Victorians: The Temperance Question in England, 1815-1872*, London, Faber and Faber, 1971, pp. 183-184, 359.

10. D. Bochel, *supra 6*; Joan F. S. King, *The Probation and After-Care Service*, London, Butterworths, 1969, pp. 2-3; David Mathieson, "The

Probation Service," in: Eric Stockdale, Silvia Casale (eds.), *Criminal Justice Under Stress*, London, Blackstone Press Ltd, 1992, pp. 141-145; Martin Page, *Crime Fighters of London: A History of the Origins and Development of the London Probation Service 1876-1965*, London, Inner London Probation Service, Benevolent and Educational Trust, 1992.

11. *The Encyclopedia Britannica: A Dictionary of Arts, Sciences, Literature and General Information*, Cambridge, The University Press, 1911, pp. 404-405; F. V. Jarvis, *Probation Officers' Manual*, London, Butterworths, 1980, pp. 50-51; David Tossell, Richard Webb, *Inside the Caring Services*, London, Edward Arnold, 1994, pp. 94-95.

12. Home Office, *Report of the Departmental Committee on the Probation Service*, Cmnd 1650, London, HMSO, 1962, par. 9.

13. Geoffrey Cartledge, "United Kingdom," in: C. G. Cartledge, P. J. P. Tak, M. Tomic-Malic, *Probation in Europe*, Hertogenbosch (The Netherland). The European Assembly for Probation and After-care, 1981, p. 474.

14. Eric Cooper, "Probation Practice in the Criminal and Civil Courts," in: John Harding, *Probation and the Community: A Practice and Policy Reader*, London, Tavistock Publications, 1987, p. 39.

15. See Chapter 6, *supra 15*.

16. M. S. Folkard et al., "Intensive Matched Probation and After-Care Treatment (IMPACT), vol. I," in: *Home Office Research Study*, 1974, 24; M. S. Folkard et al., "Intensive Matched Probation and After-Care Treatment (IMPACT), vol. II," in: *Home Office Research Study*, 1976, 36.

17. D. Haxby, *Probation, A Changing Service*, London, Constable & Co., 1978, p. 16; H. Jones, "A Case for Correction," in: *British Journal of Social Work*, 1981, 11, pp. 1-17.

18. P. Bean, "The Probation and After-Care Service in the Next Decade: Some Areas of Possible Development," in: *Justice of the Peace*, 1979, 40.

19. Peter Raynor, *Social Work, Justice and Control*, Oxford, Basil Blackwell, 1985, p. 46; Gill McIvor, "Straight Thinking About Probation," in: *Probation Journal*, 1992, 1, p. 2.

20. F. H. Wines, *Punishment and Reformation*, New York, Thomas Y. Crowell Company, 1919, p. 152.

21. N. S. Timasheff, "Probation and Imposed Peace," in: *Thought* (Fordham University Quarterly), 1941, June, p. 289.

22. C. L. Chute, M. Bell, *supra 2*, p. 33.

23. Despite common law precedents, the legality of probation was not settled until the early 1900s. In 1894, a New York district attorney challenged the judge's authority to suspend sentences, arguing that the New York statute authorizing suspension of sentence was invalid and that a common law did not apply; the New York Court of Appeals ruled in favor of the judge's right to suspend sentences; see People ex rel. Forsythe v. Court of Sessions, (1894) 36 N.E. 386. In 1916, the Supreme Court stated that neither federal nor state courts possessed the inherent power to suspend sentences permanently or indefinitely, and that common law did not apply. This decision forced each state and the federal government to legislate the power of sentence suspension; see Ex parte United States, (1916) 242 U.S. 27-53, also known as the *Killits* case.

24. Herbert G. Callison, *Introduction to Community-Based Corrections*, New York, McGraw-Hill Book Co., 1983, p. 35.

25. Presiding Judge Peter Oxenbridge Thacher of the Municipal Court of Boston set forth the nature of recognizance, as employed by him, in a subsequent case of Commonwealth v. Jerusha Chase, with term in May 1831, after the defendant, already entered into recognizance with sureties for a former offense of stealing from a dwelling house, appeared in court under another name for a new offense: "The indictment against Jerusha Chase was found at the January term of this court, 1830. She pleaded guilty to the same, and sentence would have been pronounced at that time, but upon the application of her friends, and with the consent of the attorney of the commonwealth, she was permitted, upon her recognizance for her appearance in this court, whenever she should be called for, to go at large. It has sometimes been practiced in this court, in cases of particular interest, and in the hope that the party would avoid the commission of any offense afterwards, to discharge him on a recognizance of this description. The effect is that no sentence will ever be pronounced against him, if he shall behave himself well afterwards and avoid any further violation of the law. But I cannot doubt the court may, on motion, have the party brought in and sentenced at any subsequent period. For what was the duty of the court to do at any one time, cannot cease to be its duty by delay. The judgment is postponed only, and it is in the discretion of the attorney for the commonwealth to move at any time afterwards for the appearance of the

party, according to the condition of the recognizance. In the case of Jerusha Chase, the defendant, the question is not on the validity of the recognizance, but whether the former proceedings have discharged her, so that no further judgment can be produced on the record . . . It appears, therefore, by the record, that public justice has not been satisfied, and that no punishment has been inflicted for her violation of the law in the matter whereof she stands convicted . . . By the record in this case, the defendant stands convicted of a crime, and no sufficient reason is shown why the sentence should not follow the conviction" (Horatio Woodman, ed., *Reports of Criminal Cases, Tried in the Municipal Court of the City of Boston before Peter Oxenbridge Thacher, Judge of That Court from 1823 to 1843*, Boston, The Suffolk Bar, 1845, pp. 267-270; Frank W. Grinnell, "Probation as an Orthodox Common Law Practice in Massachusetts Prior to the Statutory System," in: *Massachusetts Law Quarterly*, 1917, August, pp. 601-605). This case is important, as it is the first contemporary description of the procedure of laying on file, the unique Massachusetts term for suspending sentence under a recognizance and after a plea or verdict of guilty; it shows the revocation of a suspension after indictment for a second offense and the imposing of sentence on the original conviction.

26. (1836) 143 Massachusetts Statutes 9; F. W. Grinnell, *supra 25*, pp. 610-612; Robert M. Carter, Leslie T. Wilkins, *Probation, Parole, and Community Corrections*, New York, John Wiley & Sons, Inc., 1976, p. 84; George C. Killinger, Hazel B. Kerper, Paul F. Cromwell, Jr., *Probation and Parole in the Criminal Justice System*, St. Paul MN, West Publishing Company, 1976, pp. 2-3; John Ortiz Smykla, *Probation and Parole: Crime Control in the Community*, New York, Macmillan Publishing Co., 1984, p. 65.

27. The first experiments undertaken by Augustus, together with the first recorded use of the term probation were described in his own accounts, published ten years later: "In the month of August, 1841, I was in court one morning, when the door communicating with the lock-room was opened and an officer entered, followed by a ragged and wretched looking man, who took his seat the bench allotted to prisoners. I imagined from the man's appearance, that his offense was that of yielding to his appetite for intoxicating drinks, and in a few moments I found that my suspicions were correct, for the clerk read the complaint, in which the man was charged with

being a common drunkard. The case was clearly made out, but before sentence had been passed, I conversed with him for a few moments and found that he was not yet past all hope of reformation, although his appearance and his looks precluded a belief in the minds of others that he would ever become a man again. He told me that if he could be saved from the House of Correction, he never again would taste intoxicating liquors; there was such an earnestness in that tone, and a look expressive of firm resolve, that I determined to aid him; I bailed him, by permission of the Court. He was ordered to appear for sentence in three weeks from that time. He signed the pledge and became a sober man; at the expiration of this period of probation, I accompanied him into the court room; his whole appearance was changed and no one, not even the scrutinizing officers, could have believed that he was the same person who less than a month before had stood trembling on the prisoner's stand . . . The judge expressed himself much pleased with the account we gave of the man, and instead of the usual penalty - imprisonment in the House of Correction - he fined him one cent and costs, amounting in all to $3.76, which was immediately paid. The man continued industrious and sober, and without doubt has been by this treatment, saved from a drunkard's grave. This was truly encouraging, and before January 1842, I had bailed seventeen persons for similar offense, and they had severally been sentenced in the same manner, which in all amounted to $60.87. Eleven of this number paid the fine, but the other six being too poor to raise the amount, I paid it for them. It became a rule of this court, that a person charged with being a common drunkard, if bailed on probation, the amount of the bail should be thirty dollars, and if at the expiration of the time assigned, the person reformed, the penalty for the offense was the payment of a fine of one cent and costs of court" (John Augustus, *A Report of the Labors of John Augustus for the Last Ten Years in Aid of the Unfortunate*, Wright & Hasty, Boston, 1852, pp. 4-5, reprinted in National Probation Association, *John Augustus, First Probation Officer*, Boston, 1939).

28. Other pioneers in probation work were John M. Spear, a former clergyman and Augustus' assistant in court, George F. Haskins, founder of the first Catholic home for young offenders in New England (1851), Rufus R. Cook, the Suffolk County Jail chaplain and agent of the newly organized Children's Aid Society in the 1880s, Benjamin C. Clark and others. Christian voluntary organizations, such as The Children's Aid Society, the Society of

St. Vincent de Paul continued their work in court even after *The 1878 Act* enforced paid probation service (C. L. Chute, M. Bell, *supra 2*, pp. 53-55).

29. *The Encyclopedia Britannica, supra 11*, pp. 404-405; Louis Jankowski, *Probation and Parole 1990*, Washington DC, Bureau of Justice Statistics, 1991, p. 20.

30. Paul W. Tappan, *Crime, Justice, and Correction*, New York, McGraw-Hill Book Co., 1960, pp. 546-549.

31. David Rothman, *Conscience and Convenience*, Boston, Little, Brown & Co., 1980, pp. 82-117.

32. See *supra 23*.

33. Koichi Hamai, Renaud Ville, "Origins and Purpose of Probation," in: Koichi Hamai et al., *Probation Round the World*, London, Routledge, 1995, p. 82.

34. C. L. Chute, M. Bell, *supra 2*, pp. 18-20.

35. K. Hamai, R. Ville, supra 33, pp. 72-73.

36. United Nations, *Probation and Related Measures*, Doc. E/CN.5/230, New York, 1951, p. 54; W. Keefe, "The Adult Probation Authority in New South Wales," in: *International Journal of Offender Therapy and Comparative Criminology*, 1972, XVII, pp. 83-89.

37. N. S. Timasheff, *One Hundred Years of Probation*, New York, Fordham University Press, 1941, p. 34.

38. C. L. Chute, M. Bell, *supra 2*, pp. 29-30; J. Pratt, "The Future of the Probation Service in New Zealand," in: *The Australian and New Zealand Journal of Criminology*, 1990, XXIII, pp. 105-116; C. Eskridge, G. Nembold, "Corrections in New Zealand," in: *Federal Probation*, 1993, LVII, pp. 59-66.

39. C. L. Chute, M. Bell, *supra 2*, p. 30.

40. S. Bhattacharyya, *Probation System in India: An Appraisal*, Delhi, Manas Publications, 1986, p. 169; K. Mandal, "American Influence on Social Work Education in India and Its Impact," in: *International Social Work*, 1989, XXXII, pp. 303-309; N. Chakrabarti, "Is Rehabilitation Essential in the Probation Service in West Bengal?", in: *International Journal of Offender Therapy and Comparative Criminology*, 1992, XXXVI, pp. 121-128; H. Nagpaul, "Analysis of Social Work Teaching Material in India: The Need for Indigenous Foundations," in: *International Social Work*, 1993, XXXVI, pp. 207-220.

CHAPTER 8: CURRENT TRENDS IN THE UNITED KINGDOM

1. John L. Irwin, *Modern Britain: An Introduction*, London, Routledge, 1994, pp. 78-84.

2. Philip Priestley, *Alternatives to Crime and Punishment*, London, Channel Four Television, 1988, pp. 12-15.

3. Bill McWilliams, "Community Service National Standards: Practice and Sentencing," in: *Probation Journal*, 1989, 3, p. 124; David Tossell, Richard Webb, *Inside the Caring Services*, London, Edward Arnold, 1994, p. 96.

4. Home Office, *Supervision and Punishment in the Community*, London, HMSO, 1990.

5. Alison Jones, Brynna Kroll, John Pitts, Philip Smith, Jacqueline L. Weise, *The Probation Handbook*, Harlow-Essex, Longman, 1992, pp. 47, 106, 112.

6. There are controversial data as to the community-based disposals related to previous convictions. Probationers with previous convictions rose from 24% in 1981 to 38% in 1991, while probationers with no convictions fell from 23% to 11%. Yet community-service convicts with previous convictions fell from 40% in 1981 to 34% in 1991, while those with no convictions rose from 10% to 14% (Gordon C. Barclay, ed., *Information on the Criminal Justice System in England and Wales, Digest 2*, London, The Home Office Research and Statistics Department, 1993, p. 46).

7. Home Office, *National Standards for Probation Service, Family Court, Welfare Work*, London, HMSO, 1993, pp. 1-3.

8. The introductive chapter reads that the standards "seek to encourage good practice but avoid unnecessary prescription," although their official status remains unclear since "[i]n many respects, the standards lay down expected norms rather than outright requirements, with the clear onus on practitioners and managers to record and justify any necessary departures from these norms in individual cases" (Home Office, Department of Health, Welsh Office, *National Standards for the Supervision of Offenders in the Community 1992*, London, HMSO, 1992, p. 2).

9. Martin Wasik, Richard D. Taylor, *Blackstone's Guide to the Criminal Justice Act 1991*, London, Blackstone Press Ltd., 1991, pp. 16-18, 48-49; Home Office, *A Quick Reference Guide to the Criminal Justice Act 1991*,

London, HMSO, 1992, pp. 3-11; Andrew Ashworth, "The Criminal Justice Act 1991", in: Colin Munro, Martin Wasik (eds.), *Sentencing, Judicial Discretion and Training*, London, Sweet & Maxwell, 1992, pp. 88-89.

10. Home Office, *Probation Statistics, England and Wales*, 1992, London, The Home Office Research and Statistics Department, 1993, pp. 5-7, 17-30.

11. Home Office, *The Probation Service: Three Year Plan for the Probation Service, 1993-1996*, London, 1992, p. 2; Home Office, *The Probation Service: Three Year Plan for the Probation Service, 1994-1997*, London, 1993, p. 2; Home Office, *The Probation Service: Three Year Plan for the Probation Service, 1995-1998*, London, 1994, p. 4.

12. Bryan Gibson, Paul Cavadino, Andrew Rutherford, Andrew Ashworth, John Harding, *Criminal Justice in Transition*, Winchester, Waterside Press, 1994, pp. 37-39.

13. Home Office, *Criminal Justice and Public Order Act 1994. Introductory Guide*, London, 1994, pp. 15-16; Martin Wasik, Richard D. Taylor, *Blackstone's Guide to the Criminal Justice and Public Order Act 1994*, London, Blackstone Press Ltd., 1995, pp. 18-20.

14. E.g., in Greater Manchester area, between 1993 and 1994 the number of pre-sentence reports and probation orders rose with 5% and 20%, respectively (Andrew Underdown, Jane McLellan, Steve Robinson, Stephanie Jones, Glenda Matthews, *Performance Report, October-December 1994*, Manchester, Greater Manchester Probation Service Policy Support Unit, 1995, pp. 4, 10, 17-19).

15. Home Office, *National Standards for the Supervision of Offenders in the Community. Nearly Final Revised Drafts*, London, September 1994; Home Office, Department of Health, Welsh Office, *National Standards for the Supervision of Offenders in the Community 1995*, London, The Home Office Probation Service Division, 1995.

16. To that extent, "satisfactory compliance with the standards" should be "measured" by HM Inspectorate of Probation and the Social Services Inspectorate; offenders and other service users "should be informed of what is expected of them and the action which will be taken if they fail to comply with the requirements of the standards" (*National Standards 1995, supra 15*, pp. 1-2).

17. Home Office, *Strengthening Punishment in the Community, A Consultation Document*, Cm 2780, London, HMSO, 1995, pp. 5-6.

18. *Ibid*, pp. 19-23.

CHAPTER 9: REQUIREMENTS

Abbreviations: All E.R. = All England Law Reports; F.2d = Federal Reporter (second series); U.S. = United States Reports; U.S.C.A. = United States Code Annotated.

1. Tiberiu Dianu, "Institutia probatiunii in Marea Britanie," in: *Studii de Drept Romanesc*, 1995, 2, pp. 193-199.

2. Robert M. Carter, Leslie T. Wilkins, "Some Factors in Sentencing Policy," in: *Journal of Criminal Law, Criminology, and Police Science*, 1967, 4, p. 505; Herbert G. Callison, *Introduction to Community-Based Corrections*, New York, McGraw-Hill Book Co., 1983, pp. 104-106.

3. Andrew Ashworth, Bryan Gibson, "Altering the Sentencing Framework," in: *Criminal Law Review*, 1994, 2, p. 101; Nigel Stone, "Puzzling Section 29(1)," in: *Probation Journal*, 1994, 1, pp. 23-26.

4. Reed K. Clegg, *Probation and Parole: Principles and Practices*, Springfield IL, Charles C. Thomas Publisher, 1964, pp. 16-18.

5. Some operational studies revealed that new laws should be formulated with regard to chronic petty offenders (vagrants, drunks) that would complement their needs and limitations, since these categories seem to be immune to the process of deterrence, treatment and education. An investigation carried out in Toronto reformatories (Canada) reported that their social needs centered around work and money, while physical and psychiatric treatments scarcely mentioned, and their emotional needs included acceptance and tolerance by society, peace and stability, and they wished to conform in return (Tadeusz Grygier, "The Chronic Petty Offender: Law Enforcement or Welfare Problem?," in: *Journal of Research in Crime and Delinquency*, 1964, 2, pp. 155-167). In several U.S. states, most community penalties programs operate on a Client Specific Planning model, whose basic premise is that each offender is an individual, whose background and personal circumstances must be taken into account when designing a sentencing alternative; generally, the

program takes the form of a period of probation, payment of fines and/or restitution, and a period of community service - e.g., the North Carolina *Community Penalties Act 1983* was designed to divert from prison non-violent felons and misdemeanants facing an imminent and substantial threat of imprisonment (so called "prison-bound" offenders) for attempted burglary, forgery, receiving and possessing stolen goods, and breaking and entering a motor vehicle (Leonard Berman, Herbert Hoelter, "Client Specific Planning," in: *Federal Probation*, 1982, LXIV, p. 37; Marc Mauer, "The North Carolina Community Penalties Act: A Serious Approach to Diverting Offenders from Prison," in: *Federal Probation*, 1988, 1, pp. 11-17). In England, there are programs for burglary convicts who produced significant damages, consisting of weekly sessions, face-to-face discussions with victims, and reparations; e.g., the Rochdale burglar-victim group community program, in Greater Manchester (Greater Manchester Probation Service, *Community Options Program. Aiming for Positive Change: Burglar-Victim Group*, Rochdale, Divisional Probation Center, 1994, pp. 1-4).

6. S. Glueck, "Ten Years of Unraveling Juvenile Delinquency," in: *Journal of Criminal Law, Criminology and Police Science*, 1960, 3, pp. 253-308.

7. J. J. Cocozza, H. J. Steadman, "Some Refinements in the Measurement and Prediction of Dangerous Behavior," in: *American Journal of Psychiatry*, 1974, 9, pp. 1012-1014; J. J. Cocozza, H. J. Steadman, "The Failure of Psychiatric Predictions of Dangerousness: Clear and Convincing Evidence," in: *Rutgers Law Review*, 1976, 5, pp. 1084-1101; J. J. Cocozza, H. J. Steadman, "Prediction in Psychiatry: An Example of Misplaced Confidence in Experts," in: *Social Problems*, 1978, 3, pp. 265-276.

8. George Mair, "Some Implications of the Use of Predictive Scales by the Probation Service," in: George Mair (ed.), *Risk Prediction and Probation: Papers from a Research and Planning Unit Workshop*, Research and Planning Unit Paper 56, London, Home Office, 1989, pp. 13-14.

9. Research on sentencing procedures in 28 large American jurisdictions revealed relatively high percentages of convicted felons who were granted probation, including people convicted on burglary (25%), rape (16%), robbery (13%), and homicide (8%) charges (Mark Cuniff, *Sentencing Outcomes in Twenty-Eight Felony Courts - 1985*, Washington DC, National Institute of Justice, 1987, p. 5).

10. Sue L. Thomas, Mike Goldman, *Dangerous Offenders*, Bridgend-Mid Glamorgan (Wales), Mid Glamorgan Probation Service, 1983, pp. 1-4.

11. N. D. Walker, S. McCabe, *Crime and Insanity in England*, vol. 2, Edinburgh, Edinburgh University Press, 1973; Christopher Nuttal et al., "Parole in England and Wales," in: *Home Office Research Study*, 1977, 38.

12. Jean Floud, Warren Young, *Dangerousness and Criminal Justice*, London, Heinemann, 1981, p. 137.

13. A Wisconsin pilot study (USA), based on 7,614 cases, determined that first offenders placed on probation had lower violation rates than those imprisoned and then paroled, for probationers and parolees with one prior conviction, rates were about the same, while for those with two or more prior convictions, violation rates were higher for probationers than for parolees; offenders with low violation rates are more likely to be placed on probation, except for assault cases, where imprisonment is more frequently used (Dean V. Babst, John W. Mannering, "Probation versus Imprisonment for Similar Types of Offenders: A Comparison by Subsequent Violations," in: *Journal of Research in Crime and Delinquency*, 1965, 2, pp. 60-71).

14. Devon Probation and After-Care Committee, *Report of the Working Party on Serious Offenders*, Exeter, 1981, pp. 5-8, 37-45. There are sets of weekly session programs for violent offenders aimed at examining the links between anger violence and offending behavior by self-exploring the causes of that behavior, confronting the consequences and developing strategies for change (Greater Manchester Probation Service, *Anger Management Group*, Wigan, The Brookhouse Center, 1994, pp. 1-4; Greater Manchester Probation Service, *Community Options Program. Aiming for Positive Change: Anger Management*, Rochdale, Divisional Probation Center, 1994, pp. 1-3; Greater Manchester Probation Service, *Dealing with Conflict: The Management of Anger for Violent Offenders*, Manchester, Victoria Park Probation Center, 1995, pp. 1-3).

15. Anna Alvazzi del Frate, Maria Luisa Fornara, Andrzej Siemasko, "Etude bibliographique sur les mesures alternatives a l'emprisonnement de 1980 a 1989," in: *Revue internationale de criminologie et de police technique* (Geneve), 1991, 3, pp. 336-337.

16. David J. Bale, "Uses of a Risk of Custody Scale," in: *Probation Journal*, 1987, 4, pp. 127-131; David Bale, "The Cambridgeshire Risk of Custody Scale," in: G. Mair (ed.), *supra 8*, pp. 22-51; David Godson, "The

Use of 'Risk of Custody' Measures in Hampshire," in: G. Mair (ed.), *supra 8,* pp. 53-60; Catherine Fitzmaurice, "Predicting Risks in Courts: The Staffordshire Sentencing Prediction Scale," in: G. Mair (ed.), *supra 8,* pp. 79-105.

17. William Dodge Lewis (ed.), "Probation," in: *American International Encyclopedia. A Comprehensive Reference Work,* New York, J. J. Little & Ives Company, Inc., 1950; David M. Walker (ed.), *The Oxford Companion to Law,* Oxford, Clarendon Press, 1980, p. 1001; Henry Campbell Black (ed.), *Black's Law Dictionary,* St. Paull MN, West Publishing Co., 1991, pp. 835-836.

18. Home Office, *The Sentence of the Court: A Handbook for Courts on the Treatment of Offenders,* London, HMSO, 1969, pp. 9-10; "The Magistrates' Courts (Forms) Rules 1981, Form 64," in: *Statutory Instruments,* 1981, No. 553; Nigel Walker, *Sentencing: Theory, Law and Practice,* London, Butterworths, 1985, pp. 263-264; Home Office, *The Sentence of the Court: A Handbook for Courts on the Treatment of Offenders,* London, HMSO, 1990, p. 36; Martin Wasik, Richard D. Taylor, *Blackstone's Guide to the Criminal Justice Act 1991,* London, Blackstone Press Ltd., 1991, pp. 52-54.

19. Peter Fallon, "Crown Court Practice: Sentence," London, Butterworths, 1975, pp. 10-11.

20. A requirement of residence in a probation hostel can be for any period not exceeding the term of the probation order. Hostels provide the opportunity for a period of close supervision by hostel staff and probation officers. Emphasis is put on helping the resident through group and individual contact, both inside and outside the hostel, to move towards a more adequate way of life and away from a pattern of offending. It is possible to remand a prospective resident to a hostel for a period of 3 to 4 weeks on bail, thereby providing an opportunity to assess the offender's likely response to the regime; at the end of the period the court can decide, in light of reports received from the hostel, whether a requirement of residence in a hostel could suitably be imposed. In case some residents may be ready to leave before the end of the period of the requirement, the supervising court has the power to delete or amend the residence requirement. In England and Wales there are 81 approved probation hostels, managed by the probation service or voluntary organizations and approved by the Secretary of State. Most hostels are for

men, and some others are mixed or for women only. They are suitable for offenders with previous convictions (including imprisonment), but unlikely to be suitable for the most serious offenders, drug addicts or alcoholics who need a degree of care or containment that can be provided in other special units (Home Office, *supra 18*, 1990, pp. 36-37).

21. The probation committee may pay to the resident a maintenance allowance (a weekly sum plus a grant for clothing), when the person is required to reside in a private house other than his home (*Probation Rules 1965*, Schedule 1, par. 1/3). The period of residence is limited to the length of the probation order.

22. When a probation order requires the offender to reside in an institution which is neither an approved probation hostel, nor a hospital or other medical institution, the court must notify the terms of the order to the Secretary of State in order for inspecting such institutions; *PCCA 1973*, s. 2(8) and s. 50. Usually, a placement in a non-approved hostel is authorized if approved probation and bail hostels are inappropriate or impracticable. Also, certain voluntary organizations provide accommodation for offenders in non-approved establishments subsidized by the government (F. V. Jarvis, *Probation Officers' Manual*, London, Butterworths, 1980, pp. 50-51, pp. 61-63).

23. E.g., in Ireland for a British citizen; R. v. McCartan, (1958) 3 All E.R. 140.

24. Probation centers are defined as non-residential facilities for offenders' rehabilitation, approved by probation committees. The court must consult a probation officer and satisfy itself that arrangements for attendance can be made. Centers need the Home Secretary's approval for their functioning, in accordance with the *National Standards*. Currently, England and Wales have more than 150 probation centers with specialized programs for different types of offenders. Generally, the programs consist of working with groups and individuals, aimed at making offenders face the consequences of their actions, consider the circumstances of their offending behavior and the effects it has had on other people. Magistrates pay visits to the centers in their jurisdiction in order to see what kind of programs are available there; see Home Office, *supra 18*, 1990, pp. 37-38; M. Wasik, R. D. Taylor, *supra 18*, pp. 52-53; Bryan Gibson, Paul Cavadino, Andrew

Rutherford, Andrew Ashworth, John Harding, *Criminal Justice in Transition*, Winchester, Waterside Press, 1994, p. 149.

25. *The National Standards* recommended that probation officers should formulate a supervision plan within 10 working days of the making of the probation order as agreed to by the offender, where possible. The plan should identify the offender's relevant problems and needs, his motivation, pattern of offending and the risk of reoffending, set out the objectives for supervision and the methods to be tried in the individual program, the nature and frequency of contact and the time limits for achieving each objective. The plan should be signed by both the offender and the supervising officer, a copy given to the offender and another one held on file; it should be reviewed at least every 3 months in cooperation with the offender and amended as necessary; written records should be kept of all reviews (Home Office, Department of Health, Welsh Office, *National Standards for the Supervision of Offenders in the Community 1995*, London, The Home Office Probation Service Division, 1995, pp. 19-21).

26. *The Social Work (Scotland) Act 1968*, ss. 16, 27; *The Criminal Procedure (Scotland) Act 1975*, ss. 170, 183, 384; *The Criminal Justice (Scotland) Act 1980*, ss. 53, 54; *The Law Reform (Miscellaneous Provisions) (Scotland) Act 1990*, s. 38.

27. *CPA (Scotland) 1975*, s. 183 (4, 5, 5A), s. 384 (4, 5, 5A), as amended by *The Community Service by Offenders (Scotland) Act 1978*, s. 7, *The Mental Health (Amendment) (Scotland) Act 1983*, s. 36, *The Mental Health (Scotland) Act 1984*, part IV, and *The LR(MP)A (Scotland) 1990*, s. 38; *CJA (Scotland) 1980*, s. 58 (1) (b). See also, David M. Walker, *The Scottish Legal System: An Introduction to the Study of Scots Law*, Edinburgh, W. Green with Sweet & Maxwell Law Publisher, 1992, pp. 552-553; George Moore, Chris Wood, *Social Work and Criminal Law in Scotland*, Edinburgh, The Mercat Press, 1992, pp. 148-173.

28. F. V. Jarvis, *supra 22*, p. 82; Brice Dickson, *The Legal System of Northern Ireland*, Belfast, SLS Legal Publications, 1993, p. 203.

29. Some theorists consider the committing of a new offense as not a breach of order *per se*, but as grounds for revocation (M. Wasik, R. D. Taylor, *supra 24*, p. 61).

30. R. v. Keeley, (1960) 2 All E.R. 415.

31. W. A. Young, *Community Service Orders: The Development and Use of a New Penal Measure*, London, Heinemann, 1979, p. 66; Gill McIvor, *Sentence to Serve: The Operation and Impact of Community Service by Offenders*, Aldershot-Hampshire, Avebury, 1992, pp. 5-7.

32. Mark Drakeford, "The Probation Service, Breach and the Criminal Justice Act" 1991, in: *The Howard Journal of Criminal Justice*, 1993, 4, pp. 291-301.

33. *Probation Rules 1965*, r. 39(2); F. V. Jarvis, *supra 22*, pp. 68-69; Home Office, *supra 18*, 1990, p. 40.

34. Nick Shelley, "Early Termination of Probation: The Case Against," in: *Probation Journal*, 1993, 3, pp. 133-135.

35. Paul Cooper, Keith Moss, "Problems in Terminating Probation Orders," in: *Criminal Law Review*, 1994, 2, pp. 110-113.

36. G. Moore, C. Wood, *supra 27*, p. 185.

37. Steven H. Gifis, *Law Dictionary*, New York, Barron's Educational Series, Inc., 1991, pp. 375-376.

38. Morrissey et al. v. Brewer, Warden et al., (1972) 408 U.S. 471; Gagnon, Warden v. Scarpelli, (1973) 411 U.S. 778.

39. John P. Reed, Charles E. King, "Factors in the Decision-Making of North Carolina Probation Officers," in: *Journal of Research in Crime and Delinquency*, 1966, 2, pp. 120-128.

40. Paul W. Brown, "Morrissey Revisited: The Probation and Parole Officer as Hearing Officer," in: *Federal Probation*, 1989, 2, pp. 13-16.

41. See *supra 38*.

42. U.S. Parole Commission, *Rules and Procedures Manual*, 1987, p. 200.

43. David N. Adair, Jr., "Looking at the Law. Jurisdiction to Revoke Probation Prior to Commencement of Probation Period," in: *Federal Probation*, 1988, 1, pp. 69-70.

44. United States v. Wright, (1984) 744 F.2d 1127 (the court relied on the principle that probation could not be revoked for conduct that occurred prior to the probation period but while the defendant was on parole; because the defendant was subject to sanctions by the Parole Commission for such conduct, revocation of probation for the same conduct would interfere with the authority of the Parole Commission); United States v. Yancey, (1987) 827 F.2d 83, 87-88 (the court, upholding the authority of the court to revoke

probation for behavior occurring prior to the probation period, overruled United States v. Dick, (1985) 773 F.2d 937).

45. One of the conditions permitted in some jurisdictions as a condition of probation is a short period of incarceration, called split sentence, since part of it is served in prison and the balance on probation. Under the federal statute, (1987) 18 U.S.C.A. 3563 b.11, no more than 1 year imprisonment may be imposed as a condition of probation; see United States v. Davis, (1987) 828 F.2d 968 (defendant had received a split sentence with the recommendation that the incarceration portion of the sentence be served in a community treatment center so that he could participate in a work-release program; the court revoked probation and sentenced the defendant to 4 years incarceration for a series of non-criminal violations of institutional rules, while in the program).

46. (1987) 18 U.S.C.A. 3565.

47. United States v. Veatch, (1986) 792 F.2d 48, 51-52; United States v. Camarata, (1987) 828 F.2d 974, 980, 981 n. 13.

48. E. Latessa, C. Eskridge, H. Allen, G. Vito, *Probation and Parole in America*, New York, The Free Press, 1985.

49. Kathryn D. Morgan, "Factors Influencing Probation Outcome: A Review of the Literature," in: *Federal Probation*, 1993, 2, p. 28.

50. G. Roundtree, D. Edwards, J. Parker, "A Study of Personal Characteristics Related to Recidivism," in: *Journal of Offender Counseling Services and Rehabilitation*, 1984, 4, pp. 53-61.

51. S. Rogers, *Factors Related to Recidivism among Adult Probationers in Ontario*, Toronto, Ontario Correctional Services Ministry, 1981.

52. R. England, "A Study of Postprobation Recidivism among Five Hundred Federal Offenders," in: *Federal Probation*, 1955, XIX, pp. 10-16; J. Landis, J. Mercer, C. Wolff, "Success and Failure of Adult Probationers in California," in: *Journal of Research in Crime and Delinquency*, 1969, 6, pp. 34-40; Wisconsin Corrections Division, *Probation in Wisconsin*, Madison WI, 1972; R. Cockerill, "Probation Effectiveness in Alberta," in: *Canadian Journal of Criminology and Corrections*, 1975, 4; D. Tippman, *Probation as a Treatment Alternative for Criminal Offenders: An Analysis of Variables Related to Performance on Probation in a Sample of Men Placed on Probation*, Ph.D. dissertation, Detroit, Wayne State University, 1976; Missouri Division of Probation and Parole, *Probation in Missouri, July 1,*

1968-June 30, 1970: Characteristics, Performance and Criminal Reinvolvement, Jefferson City MO, Division of Probation and Parole, 1976; T. Bartell, W. Thomas, "Recidivist Impacts of Differential Sentencing Practices for Felony Offenders," in: *Criminology,* 1977, XV, pp. 387-396; J. Renner, *The Adult Probationer in Ontario,* Toronto, Ministry of Correctional Services, 1978; New Jersey Administrative Office of the Courts, *Adult Probation in New Jersey: A Study of Recidivism and a Determination of the Predictive Utilities of a Risk Assessment Model,* Trenton NJ, 1980; T. Holland, N. Holt, G. Beckett, "Prediction of Violent versus Nonviolent Recidivism from Prior Violent and Nonviolent Criminality," in: *Journal of Abnormal Psychology,* 1982, 91, pp. 178-182; M. Scott, H. Carey, "Community Alternatives in Colorado," in: *Criminal Justice and Behavior,* 1983, 1, pp. 93-108; G. Roundtree, D. Edwards, J. Parker, *supra 50,* pp. 53-61; M. Cuniff, *A Sentencing Postscript: Felony Probationers under Supervision in the Community,* Washington DC, National Criminal Justice Planning Association, 1986; Kathryn D. Morgan, *An Analysis of Factors Influencing Probation Outcome,* dissertation, Florida State University, 1991.

53. M. Caldwell, "Preview of a New Type of Probation Study Made in Alabama," in: *Federal Probation,* 1951, 2, pp. 3-11; G. Davis, "A Study of Adult Probation Violation Rates by Means of the Cohort Approach," in: *Journal of Criminal Law, Criminology and Police Science,* 1964, LV, pp. 70-85; D. Frease, *Factors Related to Probation Outcome,* Olympia WA, Department of Institutions, Board of Prison Terms and Parole, 1964; J. Lohman, "Ideal Supervision Caseload: A Preliminary Evaluation," in: *The San Francisco Project Research Report No. 9,* Berkeley CA, University of California School of Criminology, 1966; K. S. Ditman, "A Controlled Experiment on the Use of Court Probation for Drunk Arrests," in: *American Journal of Psychiatry,* 1967, 2, pp. 160-163; James B. Mullin, "Birth Order as a Variable of Probation Performance," in: *Journal of Research in Crime and Delinquency,* 1973, 1, pp. 29-34; Kane County Diagnostic Center, *Probation Prediction Models and Recidivism,* Geneva IL, no date; P. Kusuda, *1974 Probation and Parole Terminations,* Madison WI, Wisconsin Corrections Division, 1976; R. McGinnis, K. Klockseim, *Probation and Employment: A Report to the Bergen County,* Trenton NJ, New Jersey Probation Department, 1976; California Bureau of Statistics, *Superior Court Probation and Jail Sample,* Sacramento CA, 1977; B. McCarthy, R. Langworthy, *Older*

Offenders: Perspectives in Criminology and Criminal Justice, New York, Praeger, 1987; Joan Petersilia, "Probation and Felony Offenders," in: *Federal Probation*, 1987, 2, pp. 56-61.

54. P. Fallon, *supra 19*, p. 15; F. V. Jarvis, *supra 22*, pp. 66-67; Home Office, *A Quick Reference Guide to the Criminal Justice Act 1991*, London, HMSO, 1992, p. 32; M. Wasik, R. D. Taylor, *supra 18*, p. 62.

55. Home Office, *Wiping the State Clean*, London, HMSO, 1990, pp. 2-4; D. M. Walker, *supra 27*, p. 554.

56. Martin Wasik, Richard D. Taylor, *Blackstone's Guide to the Criminal Justice and Public Order Act 1994*, London, Blackstone Press Ltd., 1995, p. 21.

57. Currently, both probation and supervision orders can be ordered by the criminal courts for offenders aged 16 and 17 years, for a period of up to 3 years. The onus is on the court to assess the young offender's "maturity." Broadly speaking, mature 16 or 17 year olds would be more likely to receive a probation order and be supervised by a probation officer, while less mature 16 and 17 year olds are likely to receive a supervision order and be supervised by a social worker from the social services department. The distinguishing feature, pointed out by the Home Office advice, would be that the supervision order is intended to help a young person to develop into an adult, whereas a probation order is more appropriate for someone who is already emotionally, intellectually, socially and physically an adult. Any action taken to enforce the supervision order should encourage the child or young person to accept discipline but take full account of his welfare, retaining the degree of flexibility demanded by the individual's age, stage of development and degree of responsibility for his actions. Since many 16 and 17 year olds are still very much in the stage of transition into adulthood, the supervision order may often in practice be the more suitable form of supervision (Home Office, *National Standards for the Supervision of Offenders in the Community*, London, HMSO, 1992, p. 51; Home Office, Department of Health, Welsh Office, *National Standards for the Supervision of Offenders in the Community 1995*, London, The Home Office Probation Service Division, 1995, pp. 24, 30). The fact that 16 and 17 year olds can be dealt with by either the probation service or social services departments means that there must be a much closer liaison in regard to this age group. However, legally, these overlapped provisions may arbitrarily extend the role of courts in the matter.

58. S. Dickson, *supra 28*, pp. 30-31.

CHAPTER 10: CASELAW

Abbreviations: A.(2d) = Atlantic Reporter (second series); All E.R. = All England Law Reports; Cal.Rptr. = California Reporter; Cr.App.Rep. = Criminal Appeal Report; Crim.L.R. = Criminal Law Review; F.(2d) = Federal Reporter (second series); F.Supp. = Federal Supplement; L.Ed.(2d) = United States Supreme Court Reports, Lawyer's Edition (second series); N.E.(2d) = North Eastern Reporter (second series); N.W.(2d) = North Western Reporter (second series); N.Y.S.(2d) = New York Supplement (second series); P.(2d) = Pacific Reporter (second series); Q.B. = Law Reports, Queen's Bench; S.Ct. = Supreme Court Reporter; S.E.(2d) = South Eastern Reporter (second series); So.(2d) = Southern Reporter (second series); Stat. = United States Statutes at Large; U.S. = United States Reports; U.S.C. = United States Code; W.L.R. = Weekly Law Reports.

1. R. v. Cardwell, (1973) 58 Cr.App.Rep. 241.

2. D. A. Thomas, *Principles of Sentencing: The Sentencing Policy of the Court of Appeal Criminal Division*, London, Heinemann, 1979, p. 231.

3. R. v. Marquis, (1974) 59 Cr.App.Rep. 228; R. v. Barnett, (1986) 8 Cr.App.Rep. 200.

4. R. v. Percival, (1993) 15 Cr.App.Rep. 289; D. A. Thomas, *Current Sentencing Practice*, London, Sweet & Maxwell, 1994, D2-2C01, 40211.

5. R. v. Wright, (1975) Crim.L.R. 728.

6. R. v. Tarry, (1970) 2 All E.R. 185.

7. R. v. Barnes, (1986) Crim.L.R. 573.

8. R. v. Evans, (1959) 43 Cr.App.Rep. 66; R. v. Emmett, (1969) 53 Cr.App.Rep. 203; R. v. Socratous, (1984) 6 Cr.App.Rep. 33; R. v. Mullervy 8 Cr.App.Rep. 42.

9. Nigel Stone, *Probation Law. Social Work Law File, Part 3*, Norwich, University of East Anglia, 1988, p. 15.

10. R. v. Palmer, (1992) 13 Cr.App.Rep. 595.

11. R. v. Duporte, (1989) 11 Cr.App.Rep. 116.

12. R. v. Evans, *supra 8*.

13. R. v. Keeley, (1960) 44 Cr.App.Rep. 176.

14. R. v. Bradley, (1983) 5 Cr.App.Rep. 363; R. v. Adamson, (1988) 10 Cr.App.Rep. 305.

15. R. v. Peel, (1943) 2 All E.R. 95.

16. Lord Goddard CJ, *Practice direction*, (1952) 35 Cr.App.Rep. 207; for examples of breach proceedings taken for failure to be "industrious" and for "not being of good behavior" see C. Lawson, *The Probation Officer as Prosecutor*, Cambridge, Institute of Criminology, 1978, pp. 17-20.

17. The court held that a requirement to attend for a given number of hours on a given number of days at an institutional establishment (*recte* a day center) and there to comply with instructions of a wholly unspecified character given by the probation officer would go far beyond the range of such requirements as could properly be imposed under statutory provisions, on the ground both that it would involve a substantial element of custodial punishment and that it would subject the probationer to the unfettered discretionary control of the probation officer; Cullen v. Rogers, (1982) 2 All E.R. 570. As a result, *The Criminal Justice Act 1982* introduced specific powers to require attendance at a day center. Before the 1982 act, the courts used occasionally *The PCCA 1973*, s. 2(3) to insert a variety of *ad hoc* conditions, e.g., weekly baths, or bans for probationers to enter certain public houses.

18. A common format is the very open-ended condition to reside where directed by the probation officer, but not to institutions (Home Office, H.O. Circular 137/1979, London, HMSO, 1979). Such wording may confer undue discretion upon the probation officer, contrary to Cullen v. Rogers, *supra 17*. Some courts require the extra condition that the probationer shall "abide by the hostel rules," which could be deemed as a requirement "relating to the residence of the offender." If the rules were such as to give the probation officer or hotel staff "unfettered discretionary control" over the probationer, they could be objectionable, being contrary to the *Cullen v. Rogers* test.

19. R. v. Wilkinson, in: *The Times*, November 28, 1987.

20. N. Stone, *supra 9*, p. 21.

21. The Butler Committee on Mentally Abnormal Offenders, 1975, cf. N. Stone, *supra 9*, p. 21.

22. R. v. Tucker, (1974) 1 W.L.R. 615.

23. E.g., a robbery at a chemist's shop where the assistant was threatened with a knife and drugs were demanded from the pharmacist; see R. v. Heather, (1979) 1 Cr.App. Rep. 139.

24. R. v. Evans, (1961) 1 All E.R. 313.

25. R. v. Williams, (1963) Crim.L.R. 575.

26. R. v. Green, (1958) 42 Cr.App.Rep. 77, (1958) 1 All E.R. 471, (1959) 2 Q.B. 127.

27. R. v. Calvert, (1962) 2 All E.R. 1028; also, R. v. Keeley, (1960) 2 All E.R. 415 (if a fresh probation order is made but the previous order remains undischarged, though the earlier order is ineffective for the purpose of supervision, it remains in full effect for the purpose of enabling a subsequent court to impose a punishment for the offense for which it was originally made).

28. R. v. Wilcox, (1964), 2275/64, unreported, cf. Peter Fallon, *Crown Court Practice: Sentence*, London, Butterworths, 1975, p. 16.

29. R. v. Webb, (1953) 2 Q.B. 390, (1953) 37 Cr.App.Rep. 82, (1953) 1 All E.R. 1156; R. v. Fry, (1955) 1 W.L.R. 28, (1955) 38 Cr.App.Rep. 157, (1955) 1 All E.R. 21.

30. R. v. Olover and Little, (1993) Crim.L.R. 147.

31. R. v. Slatter, (1975) 3 All E.R. 215.

32. R. v. Evans, (1963) 1 Q.B. 979.

33. R. v. Crowley, (1971) 3759/A/71, R. v. Hyland (1973) 4175/C/73, cf. D. A. Thomas, *supra 2*, p. 235; R. v. Paisley, (1979) 1 Cr.App.Rep. 196; R. v. Simpson, (1983) Crim.L.R. 820; R. v. Whittingham, (1986) 8 Cr.App.Rep. 116; R. v. Tebbutt, (1988) 10 Cr.App.R. 88. The pre-1991 caselaw on breach of community orders (including probation) remained valid, once confirmed by *The CJA 1991*; s. 29(1) of the act did not treat the instant offense as more serious and deserving of punishment, since it repeated previous offending that had been treated leniently. Custody, provided as the ultimate sanction for "willful and persistent" failure to comply with a community order, is seen as an exceptional measure, since by statute the key custody threshold is the seriousness of the offense committed; *CJA 1991*, Sch. 2, par. 3(1)(d). The caselaw will likely develop on the meaning to be attributed to the term "willful and persistent;" see also *supra 14*, and Martin Wasik, Richard D. Taylor, *Blackstone's Guide to the Criminal Justice Act 1991*, London, Blackstone Press Ltd., 1991, pp. 58-60.

34. The Crown Court must hear the relevant evidence itself; the certificate of the finding of the failure by the magistrates' court is admissible but not conclusive evidence; see R. v. Holmes, (1965) 50 Cr.App.Rep. 86.

35. R. v. Thompson, (1969) 1 All E.R. 60, (1969) 52 Cr.App.Rep. 670.

36. R. v. Havant Justices, ex parte Jacobs, (1957) 1 All E.R. 475, (1957) 41 Cr.App.Rep. 62.

37. R. v. Waltham Forest Magistrates' Court, ex parte Brewer, (1991) 13 Cr.App.Rep. 405.

38. R. v. Herring, (1972) 56 Cr.App.Rep. 422.

39. R. v. Devine, (1956) 1 W.L.R. 236, (1956) 40 Cr.App.Rep. 45, (1956) 1 All E.R. 548; R. v. Holmes, (1965) 1 W.L.R. 1512, (1965) 50 Cr.App.Rep. 86, (1966) 1 All E.R. 87; R. v. Philbert (1972), 3096/A/72, (1973) Crim.L.R. 129.

40. R. v. Harrison-Jones, (1972) 2878/72 cf. D. A. Thomas, *supra 2*, p. 236.

41. R. v. Bisset, (1973) Crim.L.R. 132.

42. *Probation Rules 1984*, rules 39(1) and 39(3).

43. Burns v. United States, (1932) 287 U.S. 216, 220; Springer v. United States, (1945) 148 F.2d 411.

44. Even where federal and state statistics remain reasonably constant, the use of probation among individual judges may vary in 5% to 70% of the cases before them (Rubin, "Probation and Due Process of the Law," in: *Journal of Research in Crime and Delinquency*, 1965, 1, pp. 30-33).

45. "Some Findings from Correctional Caseload Research," in: *Federal Probation*, 1967, 53.

46. Joel Bassett, "Discretionary Power and Procedural Rights in the Granting and Revoking of Probation," in: *The Journal of Criminal Law, Criminology and Police Science* (Chicago), 1969, 4, p. 481.

47. "The Federal Probation Act 1925," Ch. 521, par. 725, in: 43 Stat. 1259.

48. E.g., the Illinois probation statute imposed *compulsory conditions* (not to violate any penal statute or ordinance of any jurisdiction, not to leave the state without the consent of the court, to appear before the court at such time as the court may direct, to execute a recognizance) and *optional conditions* (to be confined for no more than 1 year in a place other than a penitentiary, to pay a fine and/or cost of the proceedings within a period set by the court, to

make restitution or reparation to the victim, to perform or refrain from performing such other acts as may be ordered by the court); see *Illinois Statutes Annotated*, 38-110-117.2; Sklar, "Law and Practice in Probation and Parole Revocation Hearings," in: *The Journal of Criminal Law, Criminology and Police Science*, 1964, 2, p. 175.

49. People v. Baum, (Michigan, 1930) 231 N.W. 95; People v. Blankenship, (California, 1936) 61 P.2d 352 (sterilization of a syphilitic rapist, arguably a violation of the Eighth Amendment prohibition against infliction of cruel and unusual punishment); Springer v. United States, (California, 1945) 148 F.2d 411 ("donation" of blood to the Red Cross); In re Scarborough (California, 1946) 173 P.2d 825; State ex rel. Halverston v. Young, (Minnesota, 1967) 154 N.W.2d 699 (exiling probationers to further regional interests); Minnesota v. Murphy, (1984) 465 U.S. 420, 104 S.Ct. 1136, 79 L.Ed.2d 409 (the probation officer-client relationship does not hold a right of confidentiality; the probation officer could even use trickery or psychological pressure to get information and turn it over to police); Griffin v. Wisconsin, (1987) 483 U.S. 868, 107 S.Ct. 3164, 97 L.Ed.2d 709 (a probationer's home may be searched without a warrant on the grounds that the probation department "have in mind the welfare of the probationer" and must "respond quickly to evidence of misconduct").

50. Morgan v. Foster, (Georgia, 1952) 68 S.E.2d 583 (condition that probationer "maintain a correct life"); People v. Turner, (1967) 276 N.Y.S.2d 409 (condition to go to the hospital and be under medical care). Other examples of vague conditions are found in: Williams v. Harris, (Utah, 1944) 149 P.2d 640 (condition that offender "straighten up"); Swan v. State (Maryland, 1952) 90 A.2d 690 (probationer "should conduct himself in a law-abiding manner"); State v. McBride (North Carolina, 1954) 83 S.E.2d 488 (condition that "defendant be of good behavior and violate none of the laws of this state").

51. People v. Hunter, (California, 1940) 108 P.2d 472; Buhler v. Pescor, (1945) 63 F.Supp. 632; State v. Shyrock (Ohio, 1949) 89 N.E.2d 90.

52. State v. Gooding (North Carolina, 1927) 139 S.E. 436; Hollandsworth v. United States, (1929) 34 F.2d 423; City of Lima v. Beer, (Ohio, 1950) 107 N.E.2d 253; State v. White, (South Carolina, 1950) 61 S.E.2d 754; Cross v. Huff, (Georgia, 1951) 67 S.E.2d 124. *Contra*: Buhler v. Pescor, *supra 51*, 632, 638 (implied condition to act in a way "that will lead to his

rehabilitation"); Kaplan v. United States, (1956) 234 F.2d 345, 349 (directions of trial judge to make disclosures to a grand jury).

53. Whitehead v. United States, (1946) 155 F.2d 460 (implied condition not to commit a felony); Buhler v. Pescor, *supra 51*, 632.

54. For California: In re Nelson, (1921) P.947; People v. Hayden, (1950) 221 P.2d 221; In re Levi, (1951) 244 P.2d 403; People v. Slater, (1957) 313 P.2d 111; People v. Johns, (1959) 343 P.2d 92; People v. Wimberly, (1963) 30 Cal.Rptr. 421.

55. Hollandsworth v. United States, *supra 52*, 423, 427 (dictum); Redewill v. Superior Court, (Arizona, 1934) 29 P.2d 475, 479 (dictum); Varela v. Merrill, (Arizona, 1937) 74 P.2d 569, 574 (dictum); People v. Dominguez, (California, 1967) 64 Cal.Rptr. 290 (condition that robber not become pregnant while unwed).

56. Fuller v. State, (Alabama, 1899) 26 So. 146-147; Pagano v. Bechly, (Iowa, 1930) 232 N.W. 798-799.

57. (1952) 18 U.S.C. 3651; (1948) *Idaho Code Annotated* 20-222; (1956) *Nebraska Revised Statutes* 29-2219.

58. (1953) *Utah Code Annotated*, 77-35-17; (1956) *Arizona Revised Statutes Annotated*, 13-1657; In re Bine, (California, 1957) 306 P.2d 445.

59. Hollandsworth v. United States, *supra 52*, 423; Escoe v. Zerbst, (1935) 295 U.S. 490, 493.

60. Escoe v. Zerbst, *supra 59*, 490.

61. Franklin v. State, (Idaho, 1964) 392 P.2d 552; Brown v. Warden, (1965) 351 F.2d 564; Shum v. Fogliani, (Nevada, 1966) 413 P.2d 495.

62. Ex parte Lucero, (New Mexico, 1917) 168 P. 713; State v. Zolantakis, (Utah, 1927) 259 P.1044; State v. O'Neil, (Washington, 1928) 265 P. 175; Brill v. State, (Florida, 1947) 32 So.2d 607; Perry v. Williard, (Oregon, 1967) 427 P.2d 1020.

63. Cooper v. United States, (1937) 91 F.2d 195; Ex parte Boyd, (Oklahoma, 1942) 122 P.2d 162; State v. Farmer, (Washington, 1951) 237 P.2d 734.

64. State v. Greer, (North Carolina, 1917) 92 S.E. 147; Riggs v. United States, (1926) 14 F.2d 5; Jianole v. United States, (1932) 58 F.2d 115; People v. Kuduk, (Illinois, 1945) 51 N.E.2d 997; Manning v. United States, (1947) 161 F.2d 827; Blaylock v. State, (Georgia, 1953) 78 S.E.2d 537; People v. Valle, (New York, 1957), 164 N.Y.S.2d 67; People v. White, (Illinois, 1968)

239 N.E.2d 854. As indicated by these cases, the offender might never be tried for the new offense since he can be imprisoned, supposedly for his original crime, with less proof in a probation revocation proceeding.

65. State v. Barnett, (Vermont, 1939) 3 A.2d 521; People v. Becker, (Michigan, 1957) 84 N.W.2d 833. *Contra*: State v. Teal, (South Carolina, 1918) 95 S.E. 69; Swanson v. State, (Georgia, 1928) 144 S.E. 49; Ex parte Banks, (Oklahoma, 1942) 122 P.2d 181.

66. See *supra 63*; also, "Legal Aspects of Probation Revocation," in: *Columbia Law Review*, 1959, LIX, pp. 311-322; Hink, "The Application of Constitutional Standards of Protection to Probation," in: *University of Chicago Law Review*, 1962, XXIX, pp. 483-489, 495-496.

67. People v. Dudley, (Michigan, 1912) 138 N.W. 1044; Pagano v. Bechly, *supra 56*, 798; State ex rel. Jenks v. Municipal Court of City of St. Paul, (Minnesota, 1936) 266 N.W. 433; Varela v. Merrill, *supra 55*, 569; In re Weber, (Ohio, 1945) 61 N.E.2d 502; Shum v. Fogliani, *supra 61*, 495; State v. Duncan, (North Carolina, 1967) 61 N.E.2d 502.

68. Fuller v. State, *supra 56*, 146; Johnson v. Walls, (Georgia, 1937) 194 S.E. 380; Weihofen, "Revoking Probation, Parole or Pardon Without a Hearing," in: *The Journal of Criminal Law, Criminology and Police Science* (Chicago), 1942, 4, p. 531.

69. McCoy v. Harris, (Utah, 1945) 160 P.2d 721; Jones v. Cunningham, (1962) 371 U.S. 236.

70. In re Dearo, (California, 1950) 214 P.2d 585; Brown v. Warden, *supra 61*, 564; State v. Hewett, (North Carolina, 1967) 154 S.E.2d 476.

71. Burns v. United States, *supra 43*, 216; Jones v. Rivers, (1964) 338 F.2d 862; State v. Hewett, *supra 70*, 476.

72. The court did not accept the petitioner's contention that the privilege has a constitutional ground, apart from any statute, and stated that probation comes as an "act of grace to one convicted of a crime and may be coupled with such conditions in respect of its duration as Congress may impose;" but this was merely dictum because the case was reversed and remanded for failure to give the hearing required by statute; see Escoe v. Zerbst, *supra 59*, 490, 493.

73. (1944) *Florida Statutes Annotated* 948-06 (probationer advised of charges and given "opportunity to be fully heard on his behalf in person and by counsel"); (1954) *Michigan Statutes Annotated* 28-1134 (right to "a

written copy of the charges"); (1955) *Hawaii Revised Laws* 258-56, 253-5, as amended by Act 179 of 1967 (implies right to present evidence and provides right to assigned counsel); (1956) *Tennessee Code* 40-2907 (notice, right to counsel, "right to introduce testimony"); (1962) *Alaska Statutes* 33-05-070(b) ("reasonable notice" and "right to be represented by counsel"); (1964) *Minnesota Statutes Annotated* 609-14(2), 611-14(c) (right to retained counsel and assigned counsel); (1965) North Carolina General Statutes 15-200-1 (notice of charges and "a reasonable time for the defendant to prepare his defense"); (1976) Illinois Revised Statutes 38-117-3 (right to appeal); (1967) Georgia Code Annotated 27-2713 (right to counsel and to be "fully heard").

74. (1949) Iowa Code Annotated 247-26 allowed revocation "without notice" to probationer; (1958) Oklahoma Statutes Annotated 22-992 provided that probationer should be arrested and "delivered forthwith" to the place to which he was originally sentenced; (1965) Missouri Statutes Annotated 549-101 allowed revocation "without hearing."

75. In California, there is neither a constitutional nor statutory right to notice and hearing preceding revocation of probation, cf. (1954) California Penal Code 1203.1-3, and People v. Daugherty, (1965) 43 Cal. Rptr. 446, although it has been argued that a hearing is required ("Revocation of Conditional Liberty: California and the Federal System," in: South California Law Review, 1955, XXVIII, p. 158). Probation can be revoked on the report of the probation officer alone, and when a hearing is held, it may be summary in nature; see In re Levi, supra 54, 403; People v. Johns, supra 54, 92; People v. Wimberly, supra 54, 421; and the probationer has no right to present or to cross-examine witnesses; see In re Nelson, supra 54, 947; People v. Hayden, supra 54, 221; People v. Slater, supra 54, 111. Proof beyond a reasonable doubt is not necessary; see People v. Sanders, (California, 1923) 220 P. 24; People v. Johns (1959), supra 54, 92. The right to counsel is recognized where probation was granted before sentence was pronounced; the theory sustaining this rule is that the revocation proceeding is still part of the prosecution since sentence was never imposed; see In re Levi, supra 54, 401; People v. Dewaele, (California, 1964) 36 Cal.Rptr. 825; Mempa v. Rhay, (1967) 389 U.S. 128. In other California cases, the right to retained counsel appeared uncertain; see Ex parte Levi, (1952) 244 P.2d 403 (no right); People v. Wimberly, supra 54, 421 (no right); Gideon v. Wainwright, (1963) 372 U.S. 335 (probationer may be represented by counsel); People v. Walker,

(California, 1963) 30 Cal. Rptr. 440 (probationer may sometimes be represented by counsel); and the right to assigned counsel is not recognized in every court; see In re Davis, (California, 1951) 236 P.2d 579; Douglas v. California, (1963) 372 U.S. 353; Anders v. California, (1967) 386 U.S. 738. By means of a strict statutory or constitutional interpretation, many courts limited the procedural safeguards to the trial stage, although some subsequent proceedings can be prejudicial for the probationer.

76. California and Iowa allow ex parte revocation, a proceeding which does not require probationer to be present; see People v. Scott, (California, 1946) 169 P.2d 970. Oklahoma and South Dakota also permit such allowances if the breach of conditions is clearly established; see Ex parte Boyd, supra 63, 170-171; Application of Jerrel, (South Dakota, 1958) 93 N.W.2d 617; United States ex rel. Edelson v. Thompson, (1949) 175 F.2d 140.

77. Pagano v. Bechley, supra 56, 798; Varella v. Merrill, supra 55, 569; Ex parte Johnson, (Arizona, 1939) 87 P.2d 107; Ex parte Boyd, supra 63, 170-171 (dictum); In re Dearo, supra 70, 585; In re Davis, supra 75, 579; Application of Jerrel, supra 76, 614; Lint v. Bennett, (Iowa, 1960) 104 N.W.2d 564; State v. Small, (Missouri, 1965) 386 S.W.2d 379, 382.

78. (1964) 18 U.S.C. 3653 required a hearing, providing that the probationer should be "taken before the court." (1968) New York Criminal Procedure 935 required that the probationer shall have "an opportunity to be heard" by the revoking authority; see Escoe v. Zerbst, supra 59, 490; People v. Oskroba, (New York, 1953) 111 N.E.2d 235. On the other hand, (1964) California Penal Code 1203-2 provided that the authorities should arrest a probationer and "bring him before the court," but did not require a hearing; see In re Davis, supra 75, 579.

79. State v. Burnette, (North Carolina, 1917) 91 S.E. 364; State ex rel. Vadnais v. Stair, (North Dakota, 1921) 185 N.W. 301; In re Hall, (Vermont, 1927) 126 A. 24; Howe v. State ex rel. Pyne, (Tennessee, 1936) 98 S.W.2d 93; Blusinski v. Commonwealth, (Kentucky, 1940) 144 S.W.2d 1038; People v. Myers, (Michigan, 1943) N.W.2d 323; People v. Enright, (Illinois, 1947) 75 N.E.2d 777. For doctrine, see "Due Process and Revocation of Conditional Liberty," in: Wayne Law Review (Detroit), 1966, 12, p. 638.

80. Several states have statutes which explicitly provide that the hearing may be summary or informal: (1948) Idaho Code 20-222; (1953) New Jersey

Statutes Annotated 2A-168-4; (1955) New Hampshire Revised Statutes Annotated 504-4; (1958) Vermont Statutes Annotated 28-1015; (1961) Kansas General Statutes 62-2244; (1961) Oregon Revised Statutes 137-550; (1963) Louisiana Revised Statutes 15-534(c); (1966) West Virginia Code 62-12-19; (1967) Montana Revised Code 94-9831.

81. Escoe v. Zerbst, supra 59, 490; Ex parte Levi, supra 75, 403; Franklin v. State, supra 61, 552; Shum v. Fogliani, supra 61, 495.

82. Varela v. Merrill, supra 55, 569 (right to hearing and to present evidence); Ex parte Medley, (Idaho, 1953) 253 P.2d 794 (right to present evidence and cross-examine witnesses).

83. Edwardsen v. State, (Maryland, 1959) 151 A.2d 132; Thomas v. Maxwell, (Ohio, 1963) 193 N.E.2d 150; Franklin v. State, supra 61, 552; State v. Small, supra 77, 379; People v. Wood, (Michigan, 1966) 139 N.W.2d 895; Shum v. Fogliani, supra 61, 495. Contra: People v. Price, (Illinois, 1960) 164 N.E.2d 526, 534; Commonwealth ex rel. Remeriez v. Maroney, (Pennsylvania, 1964) 204 A.2d 450; Williams v. Commonwealth, (Massachusetts, 1966) 216 N.E.2d 779 (dictum); People v. Hamilton, (New York, 1966) 271 N.Y.S.2d 694; Perry v. Williard, supra 62, 1020.

84. Manning v. United States, supra 64, 827; Blaylock v. State, supra 64, 537; Bernal-Zazueta v. United States, (1955) 225 F.2d 64; Morrissey v. Brewer, (1972) 408 U.S. 471, 92 S.Ct. 2593, 33 L.Ed.2d 484 (informal inquiry required to determine if there was probable cause to believe the defendant had violated the conditions of parole and formal revocation hearing with minimum due process requirements; nota bene: the court decision detailed the procedures required for parole revocation, but because the revocations of probation and parole were similar in nature, the standards in the case affected the probation process as well; see also Chapter 9, supra 40, 41).

85. Hollandsworth v. United States, *supra 52*, 423. *Contra*: People v. Yarter, (California, 1956) 292 P.2d 649; People v. Root, (California, 1961) 13 Cal.Rptr. 209; People v. Walker, *supra 75*, 440.

86. United States ex rel. Grossberg v. Mulligan, (1931) 48 F.2d 93 (abuse of discretion in manner of interpreting probation order); Moye v. Futch, (Georgia, 1950) 60 S.E.2d 137 (failure to allow probationer to present or cross-examine witnesses); Ex parte Patterson, (Texas, 1958) 317 S.W.2d 536 (errors or irregularities which are not jurisdictional).

87. State v. Miller, (South Carolina, 1923) 115 S.E. 742; Harrington v. State, (Georgia, 1958) 103 S.E.2d 126. But: Cooper v. State, (Mississippi, 1936) 168 So. 53-54 ("evidence sufficient to convince a reasonable person").

88. Manning v. United States, *supra 64*, 792; Waters v. State, (Georgia, 1949) 55 S.E.2d 677; Reinmuth v. State, (Nebraska, 1957) 80 N.W.2d 874; People v. Koning, (Illinois, 1958) 151 N.E.2d 103.

89. People v. Turner, *supra 50*, 409.

90. People v. Dudley, *supra 67*, 1044; Burns v. United States, *supra 43*, 216.

91. (1962) U. S. Model Penal Code 301-4 provided that: "The Court shall not revoke a suspension or probation or increase the requirements imposed thereby on the defendant except after a hearing upon written notice to the defendant of the grounds on which such action is proposed. The defendant shall have the right to hear and controvert the evidence against him, to offer evidence in his defense and to be represented by counsel." In Mempa v. Rhay, *supra 75*, 128, the court unanimously held that a probationer was constitutionally entitled to counsel in a revocation-of-probation proceeding where the imposition of sentence had been suspended. Prior to *Mempa*, a probationer was not entitled to be represented or assisted by counsel at the revocation proceedings.

92. People v. Oskroba, *supra 78*, 235; Dingler v. State, (Georgia, 1960) 113 S.E.2d 496; People v. Price, *supra 83*, 528, 533; Crenshaw v. State, (Maryland, 1960) 161 A.2d 669. Generally, notice requirements at revocation proceedings are less strict than at other judicial proceedings; see Jianole v. United States, (1932) *supra 64*, 115. The courts tend to regard the hearing and notice requirements as one issue because the hearing is inadequate if proper notice was not given; see Sellers v. State, (Nebraska, 1921) 181 N.W. 862; People v. Hodges, (Michigan, 1925) 204 N.W. 801; Slayton v. Commonwealth, (Virginia, 1946) 38 S.E.2d 479.

93. In re Levi, *supra 54*, 403; Edwardsen v. State, *supra 83*, 132, 136; People v. Price, *supra 83*, 528, 534; Thomas v. Maxwell, *supra 83*, 150, 152; People v. Hamilton, *supra 83*, 694; Williams v. Commonwealth, *supra 83*, 779; People v. Wood, *supra 83*, 895; Perry v. Williard, *supra 62*, 1020; Gagnon v. Scarpelli, (1973) 411 U.S. 778, 93 S.Ct. 1756, 36 L.Ed.2d 656 (both probationers and parolees have a constitutionally limited right to counsel in revocation proceedings); the *Gagnon* case can be viewed as a step forward in the application of constitutional safeguards to the correctional

process in the sense that provides some control over the unlimited discretion exercised in the past by probation and parole personnel in revocation proceedings.

94. People v. Enright, *supra 79*, 777; Mason v. Cochran, (Mississippi, 1950) 46 So.2d 106; Fiorella v. State, (Alabama, 1960) 121 So.2d 875, 878.

95. Robinson v. State, (Georgia, 1940) 8 S.E.2d 698; City of Lima v. Beer, *supra 52*, 253; People v. Oskroba, *supra 78*, 235.

96. United States ex rel. Grossberg v. Mulligan, *supra 86*, 93; Huff v. Diebold, (Kentucky, 1950) 233 S.W.2d 276; People v. Turner, *supra 50*, 409. *Contra*: People v. Gregory (1967) 1 Criminal Law Reports 2266.

97. J. Bassett, *supra 46*, p. 491.

98. Gideon v. Wainwright, *supra 75*, 335; In re Gault, (1967) 387 U.S. 1.

99. Burns v. United States, *supra 43*, 216; Escoe v. Zerbst, *supra 59*, 490; Ohio Bell Telephone Co. v. Commission, (1937) 301 U.S. 292, 302 (the court characterized the "protection of the individual against arbitrary action" as the very essence of the due process clause).

100. Mapp v. Ohio, (1961) 367 U.S. 643; Miranda v. Arizona, (1966) 384 U.S. 436.

101. Townsend v. Burke, (1948) 334 U.S. 736; Mempa v. Rhay, *supra 75*, 128.

102. United States v. Carson, (1982) 669 F.2d 216.

103. (1982) 31 Cr.L. 2081, cf. Joseph J. Senna, Larry J. Siegel, *Introduction to Criminal Justice*, St. Paul MN, West Publishing Company, 1993, p. 541.

CHAPTER 11: LEGAL REFORM IN TRANSITION SOCIETIES

1. Tiberiu Dianu, "The Value of Foreign Training for Law Reform and Judicial Restructuring in Romania," in: *Revue Roumaine des Sciences Juridiques*, 1993, 2, pp. 208-209.

2. Stanislaw Frankowski, Paul Stephan, "Westernization of the European East?," in: Stanislaw Frankowski, Paul B. Stephan (eds.), *Legal Reform in Post-Communist Europe: The View from Within*, Dordrecht, Martinus Nijhoff Publishers, 1995, pp. 480-482.

3. In Poland, the 1969 Penal Code imposed on offenders released on license a 2-to-5-year placement in "centers for social readaptation" followed by a 3-to-5-year "protective supervision", depending upon their rehabilitation needs. Such a double-track system, similar in a way to U.S. boot camps, was

in daily practice unduly harsh and ineffective, and subsequently abolished in 1990 (Andrzej Wasek, Stanislaw Frankowski, "Polish Criminal Law and Procedure," in: S. Frankowski, P. B. Stephan, *supra 2*, p. 291; Zbigniew Holda, "The Law of Corrections in Poland," in: S. Frankowski, P. B. Stephan, *supra 2*, p. 363). In Russia, the moderate humanization of the correctional system between 1969-1971 did not bring lower rates of recidivism but a more hostile public attitude toward the liberal trends in the treatment of offenders (Alexander S. Mikhlin, "The Law of Corrections in Russia," in: S. Frankowski, P. B. Stephan, *supra 2*, pp. 332, 341-342). In Romania, "rehabilitation" was made merely by passing amnesty and pardon decrees or by placing offenders under lay supervision of some collectives of workmates. Also, in the early 1970s, funds for education were severely curbed, and the sociology classes in the universities, designed to train social workers, were canceled (Tiberiu Dianu, "The Romanian Criminal Justice System and the Reform Movement in a Transition Society," in: *Revue Roumaine des Sciences Juridiques*, 1994, 1, p. 54). In Hungary, the social care services of the late 1970s had some success in the offender's rehabilitation but later on the offensive of the retributive philosophies blurred the rehabilitative ideals (Bela Busch, Jozsef Molnar, Eva Margitan, "Criminal Law, The Law of Criminal Procedure, and The Law of Corrections in Hungary," in: S. Frankowski, P. B. Stephan, *supra 2*, pp. 249-251).

4. After 1989, most of the East European states adjusted their statutes to the UN, the Council of Europe and the European Convention on Human Rights standards. For Bulgaria, see Ekaterina Trendafilova, "Criminal Procedure in Bulgaria," in: S. Frankowski, P. B. Stephan, *supra 2*, p. 313; for Hungary, see B. Busch, J. Molnar, E. Margitan, *supra 3*, p. 252; for Poland, see A. Wasek, S. Frankowski, *supra 3*, pp. 304-305; Z. Holda, *supra 3*, pp. 363-364; for Romania, see Rodica-Mihaela Stanoiu, Tiberiu Dianu, "Reform Movements in Criminal Procedure and the Protection of Human Rights," in: *Revue Roumaine des Sciences Juridiques*, 1992, 2, pp. 190-191; Tiberiu Dianu, "The Romanian Criminal Justice System," in: S. Frankowski, P. B. Stephan, *supra 2*, pp. 260-261.

5. The "dual humanism" theorists believe that mercy should apply both to offender and society; therefore, giving a tougher treatment for the offender, whose weak personal responsibility contributes to a higher crime rate, should be also regarded as a proof of humanism. Other supporters view harsh

punishments as applicable solely to the most serious offenders (A. S. Mikhlin, *supra 3*, p. 342).

6. The "humanized retribution" theory operates with four principles: rule of law, mutual respect between prison staff and inmates, minimum isolation in prisons and further integration of the correctional system with the outside social environment (Z. Holda, *supra 3*, pp. 357-358).

7. In Romania, the death penalty was abolished by law-decree in January 1990 but press campaigns favoring its reinstatement emerged in 1993. The legislators eventually blocked reinstatement initiatives, fearing that Romania would face opposition to her request to join the Council of Europe (Tiberiu Dianu, "The Evolution of Capital Punishment in Romania," in: *Revue Roumaine des Sciences Juridiques*, 1995, 2, p. 188-189; T. Dianu, *supra 4*, p. 262).

8. E.g., in Romania, the Penal Code, Art. 53(1), as amended by Law no. 140 of November 5, 1996, enhanced the upper limit of imprisonment from 25 years to 30 years.

CHAPTER 12: OPTIONS FOR A PUNISHMENT REFORM

1. John DiTulio, Charles Logan, "The Ten Deadly Myths About Crime and Punishment in the U.S.," in: *Wisconsin Interest*, 1992, 1, pp. 21-35.

2. Josine Junger-Tas, *Alternatives to Prison Sentences: Experiences and Developments*, Amsterdam, Kugler Publications, 1994, p. 81.

3. James Byrne, Linda Kelly, *Restructuring Probation as an Intermediate Sanction: An Evaluation of the Massachusetts Intensive Probation Supervision Program*, Washington DC, National Institute of Justice, 1989; Todd Clear, Patricia Hardyman, "The New Intensive Supervision Movement," in: *Crime and Delinquency*, 1990, XXXVI, pp. 42-66; Norval Morris, Michael Tonry, *Between Prison and Probation: Intermediate Punishments in a Rational Sentencing System*, New York, Oxford University Press, 1990, pp. 237-241; Doris Layton MacKenzie, "The Parole Performance of Offenders Released from Shock Incarceration (Boot Camp Prisons): A Survival Time Analysis," in: *Journal of Quantitative Criminology*, 1991, 3, pp. 213-236; J. J. Senna, L. J. Siegel, *Introduction to Criminal Justice*, St. Paul MN, West Publishing Company, 1993, p. 547; J. Junger-Tas, *supra 2*, p. 86.

4. If the American experts' enthusiasm for the future of the new alternatives resides in their paternity for those devices, their British counterparts display a rather moderate optimism (Andrew Wade, *The Electronic Monitoring of Offenders*, Norwich, Social Work Monographs, 1988, pp. 37-41; David Hill, *Intensive Probation Practice: An Option for the 1990s*, Norwich, Social Work Monographs, 1991, pp. 28-29; Ian D. Brownlee, Derrick Joanes, "Intensive Probation for Young Adult Offenders: Evaluating the Impact of a Non-Custodial Sentence," in: *The British Journal of Criminology*, 1993, 2, p. 228; George Mair, Charles Lloyd, Claire Nee, Rae Sibbitt, *Intensive Probation in England and Wales: An Evaluation*, Home Office Research Study No. 133, London, HMSO, 1994, pp. 123-124), and even skepticism (George Mair, Claire Nee, *Electronic Monitoring: The Trials and Their Results*, Home Office Research Study No. 120, London, HMSO, 1990, pp. 67-68; Philip M. Lloyd, *Balancing European and North American Criminal Justice*, Manchester, Rhodes Foundation Scholarship Trust, 1995, pp. 8-10); skeptics invoke lack of national support (*recte* the plain opposition these devices face from the probation services) and, in relation to that, the reluctance for high-tech approaches in working with offenders (impersonal electronic methods are deemed by far as less effective than personalized supervision).

5. Joan Petersilia, *Expanding Options for Criminal Sentencing*, Santa Monica CA, Rand Corporation, 1987, p. 32; Edward Latessa, Gennaro Vito, "The Effects of Intensive Supervision on Shock Probationers," in: *Journal of Criminal Justice*, 1988, 16, pp. 319-330; James Beck, Jody Klein-Saffran, Harold Wooten, "Home Confinement and the Use of Electronic Monitoring with Federal Parolees," in: *Federal Probation*, 1990, LIV, pp. 22-31; Annette Jolin, Brian Stipak, "Drug Treatment and Electronically Monitored Home Confinement: An Evaluation of a Community-Based Sentencing Option," paper presented at: *The Annual Meeting of the American Society of Criminology*, San Francisco, November 1991.

6. Stephen Gettinger, "Intensive Supervision: Can It Rehabilitate Probation?," in: *Correction Magazine*, 1983, 9, pp. 7-18.

7. The prison cost per inmate ranges between US$ 15,000-30,000 per year, the cost of probation runs about US$ 2,000 per year (US$ 6,000 per year in some jurisdictions), while electronic monitoring and intensive probation supervision programs range between US$ 3,000-6,000 per year; see V. Fogg,

"Expanding the Sanction Range of ISP Programs: A Report on Electronic Monitoring," in: *Journal of Offender Monitoring*, 1990, 3, pp. 12-13, 16, 18; Frank Pearson, Alice Glasel Harper, "Contingent Intermediate Sentences: New Jersey's Intensive Supervision Program," in: *Crime and Delinquency*, 1990, XXXVI, pp. 75-86; Joan Petersilia, "An Evaluation of Intensive Probation in California," in: *Journal of Criminal Law and Criminology*, 1992, LXXXII, p. 648; Sam Howe Verhovek, "Texas Caters to a Demand Around U.S. for Jail Cells," in: *The New York Times*, February 9, 1996, p. A1; Roberto Suro, "More Is Spent On New Prisons Than Colleges: Institute Urges Change In Funding Priorities," in: *The Washington Post*, February 24, 1997, p. A12; William Raspberry, "Sermon on a Bus: Touring Rich Schools, Poor Schools and the Costliest School of All: Prison," in: *The Washington Post*, March 7, 1997, p. A21.

8. James Byrne, "The Future of Intensive Probation Supervision and the New Intermediate Sanction," in: *Crime and Delinquency*, 1990, 1; Michael Tonry, Richard Will, *Intermediate Sanctions*, Washington DC, National Institute of Justice, 1990, p. 8; J. J. Senna, L. J. Siegel, *supra 3*, p. 542; J. Junger-Tas, *supra 2*, p. 88.

INDEXES

AUTHOR INDEX

NOTE - References are to chapter notes; *e.g.*, "1.2" reads "Chapter 1, note 2." Institutions are printed in capitals. Due to variation of first name initials, same authors may occasionally appear on separate entries.

CASE INDEX